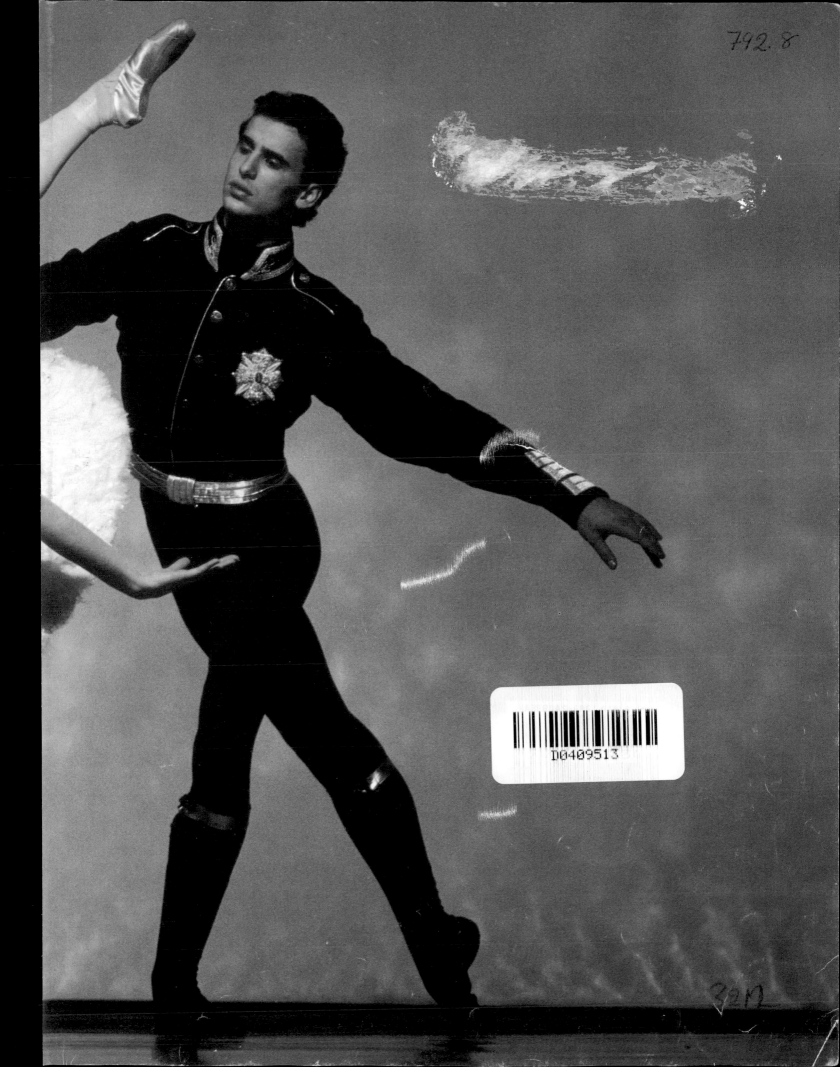

DK SUPERGUIDES
BALLET

Dancing together

Thread and scissors for repairs

An attitude

Folk dancing

Standing in fifth position

Learning to tie shoe ribbons

DK SUPERGUIDES

BALLET

DARCEY BUSSELL

with
Patricia Linton

An advanced jump

Flat leather shoes

On pointe

Cotton and shoe ribbons

Making up

Putting on a show

DK

DORLING KINDERSLEY
London • New York • Sydney • Delhi

DK www.dk.com

A DORLING KINDERSLEY BOOK

DK www.dk.com

Project editor Louise Pritchard   **Art editor** Carole Orbell
Special photography Liz McAulay and John Garrett
Production Catherine Semark
Deputy editorial director Sophie Mitchell
Deputy art director Miranda Kennedy

The young dancers
Georgina Broadhurst, Lara Glew, Robert Gravenor, Elizabeth Holliday, Oliver Lewis,
Nandita Shankardass, Lisa Todd, Anna Totesaut, Alex Whitley

This revised edition published in Great Britain in 2000 by
Dorling Kindersley Limited
9 Henrietta Street, London WC2E 8PS
First published as *The Young Dancer*, 1994

2 4 6 8 10 9 7 5 3 1

A CIP catalogue record for this book is available from the British Library

ISBN 0 7513 2800 6

Colour reproduction by Colourscan, Singapore
Printed and bound in Italy by L.E.G.O.

Contents

6
To all young dancers

8
Getting ready to dance

10
Starting ballet

12
Basic positions

14
Pliés and relevés

16
Battement tendu

18
Battement fondu

20
Further exercises

22
Bending

24
Using your arms

26
Classical ballet poses

28
Arabesques

30
Linking movements

32
Pirouettes

34
First jumps

36
Bigger jumps

38
On your toes

40
Advanced pointework

42
Pas de deux

44
Folk and character dancing

46
Mime and make-up

48
Preparing for a show

50
The show

52
My life as a ballet dancer

54
Other dance forms

56
Choreography

58
Going to the ballet

60
Useful addresses

61
Details of a selection of ballets

62
Glossary

64
Index
&
Acknowledgments

To all young dancers

" **D**ANCE IS a wonderful art and one of the few where we are the actual material from which it is created. When I was five years old I started going to ballet classes on Saturday mornings with my friends. I did not think about it as a career until I was 13 years old. Ballet classes sometimes seemed very strenuous and repetitive, but I now appreciate persevering with my training. The rewards I have had from performing are truly amazing. I hope you enjoy reading this book and that it helps you to persevere too. "

Poise, line, and beauty are developed in the art of classical ballet.

You will need to train correctly, even for the simplest movements.

When on pointe, you will need to work for lightness and delicacy.

These satin shoes and ribbons are pretty. But don't be deceived. You need stamina and endurance if you want to be a ballet dancer.

You may learn joyful folk and character dances in your classes.

Strength, poise, and balance are very important when jumping.

Because dance is so demanding, you will do special exercises to build up your strength.

It is fun to work together. Helping someone else with their technique will also help you to develop your own.

The tradition of ballet

As an art, ballet in Europe originated in the 15th and 16th centuries in the lavish court entertainments, known as masques. Through the work of dedicated teachers, its traditions have been handed down to students year after year, and developed by each generation. In order to dance beautifully, you need to feel and understand the tradition of ballet. Try to learn and appreciate it for yourself and feel that you are a part of it. Your dancing will grow and develop in feeling if you know about other arts, too, such as music and painting. Sensitivity to different forms of beauty, including that of nature, can only make you more sensitive to beauty in ballet.

Carlotta Grisi, one of the greatest ballerinas of the Romantic period (the first half of the 19th century).

Pas de deux requires years of specialized training. By starting with simple poses such as this, you may eventually come to perform in some of the great masterpieces.

Ballet today

The love of ballet is not confined to a particular place or time. People all over the world appreciate it and enjoy its lightness and grace. It speaks through movement straight to the heart and eye. Because ballet is a living art which is always developing, today's dancers and choreographers create new ballets as well as present the classics. I gain great pleasure from dancing and enjoy the fact that I am still learning all the time.

When you choreograph your own ballets, your imagination is free to explore music and ideas. Creating a theatrical presentation can be inspiring as well as great fun.

I have been able to dance in great ballets such as Swan Lake because of good training and hard work.

Getting ready to dance

ON STAGE, especially in the older ballets, costumes are full and lavish, but our practice clothes are quite different. In a ballet class, where you learn and practise before going on to the stage, you will concentrate on exactness of line and movement. The clothes that you wear are designed with this in mind. They are practical and uncluttered. You must be able to move and stretch easily and your teacher must be able to see exactly what you are doing.

You should have tidy hair so that it does not fall in your eyes or irritate you.

T-shirt

Leotard

Tights

Spare elastic

Pins and grips for keeping hair tidy

Small sewing kit for last-minute repairs

Spare ribbon

Tidy box
It is important for you to be well organized and arrive at class with everything that you need. It is a good idea to have a box in which you can keep all your useful bits and pieces.

Clothes for girls
The best thing for you to wear in class is a simple leotard. Sometimes you may wear a short skirt over it. It is best if you wear socks, not tights, until you are about 11 or 12 years old. When you have bare legs, your teacher will be able to see that your muscles are working correctly as you learn all the movements. You can wear leather, canvas, or satin flat shoes with elastic or ribbons. Later you can wear satin pointe shoes with ribbons.

Satin flat shoes

Clothes for boys
To start with you should wear trunks over a vest or leotard, and socks. Later you will wear tights with a leotard or T-shirt, or all-over-body tights. Boys wear leather or canvas shoes with elastic.

Canvas shoes

Tidy hair
Make sure your hair is tidy and off your face for your class. For girls, it is ideal if your hair is long enough to put up – about shoulder length. Ask a friend to help you if you find it difficult to begin with. If your hair is too short to put up, it doesn't matter. Just pin or tie it back securely.

Sewing on the elastic
To find the right place to sew on your elastic or ribbon, fold the heel of your shoe over. The crease that is made at the side of the shoe is about the right place. Angle the elastic or ribbon slightly towards the toe and sew 2 cm into the shoe. Sew one ribbon in each side, or measure the elastic over your foot and allow another 2 cm to sew in the other side.

Do not sew through the drawstring.

Remove all jewellery
Do not wear jewellery in class. Earrings are dangerous and a watch might scratch someone, or snag tights or leotards.

Ready-made tutu

Footwear
It is best to go to a specialist shoe shop to have your shoes fitted properly. Shoes should not be too loose or too tight. They should fit like a glove. Your feet, especially your toes, must be able to work freely while the shoes feel quite snug and secure. Unless your teacher asks you to buy more, buy only one pair of shoes at a time, because your feet are growing all the time.

Darning pointe shoes
Don't buy pointe shoes until your teacher asks you to. This will not be until you have studied hard for several years. When you do buy them, you can make them last longer by darning the ends.

Alternative outfits
A tutu may be suitable for girls to wear on a special occasion. Tutus that you see professional dancers wearing on stage take a long time to make because they are specially sewn and fitted. You can buy a ready-made one from a specialist shop. It will be simple but very pretty and you will look lovely for a special performance.

Use the drawstring to adjust the fit round the top of your shoe. Then tuck in the ends.

Putting shoes away
Check to see if your shoes need to be cleaned or repaired after a class. Fold each shoe neatly, then wrap any ribbons around and tuck in the ends. Keep all your dance shoes together in a bag.

How to tie ribbons

1 It is important that you tie your ribbons properly. They have to be just right to be comfortable and neat. Your teacher will help you until you have learned how to do it. Take the inside ribbon first and pass it across and around your ankle.

You will need about 105 cm of ribbon for one pair of shoes.

2 Continue taking this ribbon round the front of your ankle. Keep it quite taut so that it does not wrinkle, but not so tight that it pinches.

3 Now pass this ribbon around the back again. Pick up the outside ribbon, being careful not to let the first ribbon slip down.

Ribbons can be made of nylon or satin.

4 Pass the outside ribbon over and round your ankle. Keep the ribbons close together, one on top of the other. Remember, your ribbons can support you, but must not restrict the movement of your feet.

5 Bring the ribbons together on the inside of your foot and tie them in a neat knot, slightly away from your ankle. Don't cut the extra ribbon off until you are sure you feel comfortable. Leave yourself about 4 or 5 cm after the knot.

6 Tuck in the knot and the ends to leave the ribbons looking neat and tidy. Bits of ribbon that escape while you are dancing are often called "pigs' ears".

Starting ballet

BALLET IS an art which can be very beautiful, expressive, and dramatic. So much can be brought to life – comedy, tragedy, love, humour, and joy. It began in the Italian courts in the 15th century. The princes put on spectacles that included poetry, music, singing, and dancing. Ballet grew as a separate dance form and set steps and professional ballet dancers began to appear in the 17th century. King Louis XIV of France was a keen dancer and France became the first centre of the ballet world. This is why the language of ballet is in French to this day. In a ballet class you will study rules which have been laid down over the centuries. It will be hard work, but you will be entering a rich and fulfilling tradition.

Mirrors are helpful for you to check your position.

Studios

Ballet studios can be any shape or size. There should be a barre around the walls for you to hold during the exercises at the beginning of class. The floor may be made of wood or vinyl. The surface of some studio floors is specially made to "give" a little as you jump. This is more comfortable to work on.

Dedicated training

To become a professional ballet dancer you will need determination, strength, a good teacher, and whole-hearted dedication. Even now I am a ballerina, I still need to discipline myself to a daily training routine.

Early exercises

In your first classes you will learn ballet steps slowly and carefully. You will also learn various movements to help you with musicality and coordination. These are based on natural movements such as walking, running, skipping, and jumping.

Move with the music

In ballet classes a pianist will work closely with your teacher. You must learn to feel the music and to express what you feel in the way you move. Musicality is vital in a dancer.

Look straight ahead.

If there are two barres, use the one that is most comfortable for you.

Keep your shoulders open and lowered.

Placing

In classical ballet your body needs to be correctly placed to help you find the necessary light and lifted qualities. In this preparatory exercise for placing, face the barre with your hands lightly on it, your elbows relaxed and slightly in front of your body.

Pull up the muscles in your bottom, legs, and tummy.

Strengthening your feet

This is a good exercise to do before class to warm up your feet and ankles. It helps you to work on the use of your feet and to feel a lengthening down the back of your legs.

Flex and stretch your feet, keeping a straight line through your legs and feet.

Your spine is the centre of your balance. Feel that your body is straight.

Different methods

There are many different approaches to teaching ballet. The important thing is for you to have a clear and logical development which takes you from the simple to the complex with precision and quality.

Boys and girls

In the first few years of training, boys' and girls' steps are almost the same. Boys will emphasize strength and manliness; girls will work for lightness and delicacy. Both must strive for balance and poise.

You will need to develop turned-out legs, suppleness, and coordination.

A ballet dancer needs strength, delicacy, grace, taste, and knowledge.

Centre practice

You should practise good placing without the barre in the centre, too, before learning the five positions of the feet and arms, and basic classical movements. It is important that you understand and place each shape correctly and dance it with the right feeling. Your teacher and the music will help you to do this.

Révérence

The formal way to say thank you in ballet is called a *révérence*. You will do it at the end of each class to thank your teacher, pianist, or any visitors. It is sometimes performed at the beginning of class, too, to mark your entry into the world of ballet. One day you will make your *révérence* to thank the audience for their applause.

Girls place one foot behind and bend their knees in révérence.

Boys finish their révérence standing naturally, but poised, with their head bowed.

11

Basic positions

E VERY NEW STEP you learn will make use of the basic positions. All dancers, even the greatest, use exactly these positions every day. They may be able to perform the most beautiful and expressive steps, but they are still using these shapes. It is vital that you understand and perform the five turned out positions of the feet well, and feel safe and secure in them. You will use them at the beginning and end of movements, and in passing from one movement to another. An insecure start and finish to a movement is uncomfortable for both dancer and audience. You must concentrate hard when you are learning these positions because as you get older, and your classes become more complicated, it will be difficult for you to correct mistakes in your basic work.

Dance with feeling
Your basic positions must be performed correctly and precisely, but also danced with feeling and expression.

This is the preparatory position for your arms. You will begin the movement to all the other arm positions from here.

Epaulement
Almost from the start of your training, you will learn how to turn your body a little towards or away from the audience. This is called *épaulement*. With this slight turn of your body, you look quite different from standing *en face*. It softens the line of your body and gives you a more refined look. This is your first glimpse of how a basic shape can be artistically transformed.

You will learn the five positions of the feet facing the barre, then sideways to the barre, and finally in the centre. The positions are shown here en face, *or facing the front.*

Positions of the feet

First position
Turn your toes out to the side with your heels touching. You must turn your whole leg out at the hip, not just your foot. At first you may not be able to turn out very far. You will improve after some hard work.

Second position
Turn your toes out on the same line as first position, but stand with your feet apart. The space between your heels should be about the length of one of your feet. Place the whole of both feet on the floor. Don't roll forwards and put too much weight on your big toes.

Positions of the arms

Keep your side arm just in front of the line of your shoulders.

3 Hold one arm curved in front of you and the other arm out to the side. To help you keep the right shape, imagine that something is gently supporting your little fingers and your elbows.

4 Take one arm up and hold it in a graceful curve, slightly in front of your head. Your other arm should be out to the side, also gently curved. In all these positions keep your tummy muscles pulled up as well as the muscles of your bottom. Keep your back straight and your shoulders open and lowered.

1 Hold your arms in front in an oval shape. Your hands should be curved and your fingers grouped elegantly and naturally. Curve in your middle fingers slightly more than the others. Relax your thumbs so that they do not stick up.

Keep a rhythm
Move smoothly from one position to the next.

2 Open your arms wide, but keep them in front of your shoulders. Hold them slightly curved and be careful not to drop your elbows. Try to keep your fingers delicate and soft.

5 Take both arms up and hold them in an oval shape, framing your face. Do not let your shoulders lift with your arms. Without looking up, you should be aware of your fingers slightly in front of your head.

Pull up your body
Always keep your body well lifted, or "pulled up". You will then find it easier to turn your legs out in the hip joints. It will also help you to look and feel light and secure.

The distance between your feet should be about the length of one of your feet.

Third position
Cross one foot halfway in front of the other. Don't forget it is not just your feet that must work. Keep your legs turned out and your body lifted. Your weight should be balanced evenly on both legs.

Fourth position
This is the most difficult position, because it is hard to maintain your turnout. Place one foot exactly in front of the other with a space between them.

Fifth position
You will study this position when you have learned to hold yourself well, and your feet and legs are strong. Your feet should be turned out, fully crossed, and touching each other firmly.

Pliés and reléves

T HE ORDER of exercises that you do in your ballet class has been developed over generations to give your body and mind the right preparation to dance. At first your class will be quite slow and simple, but simple does not mean mechanical or like a robot. Even simple steps should be done artistically, intelligently, and musically. Each step has its own quality that gives it a life of its own. *Pliés* (*plier* meaning to bend or fold) and *reléves* (*relever* meaning to raise) are the first movements you will learn. They are also the foundation of almost every movement in classical dance.

Preparation of the arm

Place your inside hand lightly on top of the barre, a little in front of your body.

1 When you have learned a movement facing the barre, turn sideways and stand with your free arm in preparatory position. During the musical introduction before the exercise begins, prepare your arm. As the music starts, take a breath to lift and lighten your body. With this breath, slightly open your free arm, starting with your fingertips.

Plié in first

Holding the barre
Keep your hands exactly opposite your shoulders with your elbows down.

Improve with practice
Part of the work of a dancer is to repeat steps and make them look and feel better each time.

Keep your back strong.

In demi-plié, your heels must always stay on the floor.

1 *Pliés* are ideal for preparing your body at the start of class. Stand facing the barre with your legs stretched, your shoulders and hips level, and your body lifted.

2 Bend your knees and try to increase the turnout in the upper part of your legs. Without taking your heels off the ground, go as far as your ankles will allow.

3 To continue into *grand plié*, gradually let your heels lift a little as you go down all the way. Bend your knees until your thighs are parallel with the floor. Coming up, replace your heels as soon as you can without forcing them.

Pliés in the centre

It is harder to balance and hold your turnout without the barre. Even so, you will soon try each new step in the centre. Feel your muscles holding the shape exactly as you did at the barre. *Grands pliés* in fourth and fifth positions are even more difficult and you will not be asked to try these until you are quite advanced.

Grand plié in fourth

Grand plié in fifth

2 Pass your hand back through preparatory to first position. Following your hand with your eyes, open your arm to second position.

Relevé in first position

1 This movement will help you to develop strength and flexibility in your legs and feet. Place your feet evenly on the floor. This is very important.

2 Smoothly lift both your heels off the floor at the same time. Keep your knees taut and try hard to hold your turnout. Keep your tummy and back muscles strong.

3 Continue to rise to *demi-pointe*. Think about "gathering" yourself up and feeling your balance. Slowly lower your heels again. Try to feel a line through the centre of each foot so that you work both sides evenly.

It is dangerous to lean on either your big or little toes.

Plié in second

Never let your knees fall inwards. They must always look over your toes.

Work both sides equally.

Keep very straight as your knees bend and stretch.

1 This exercise will help you to gain strength and elasticity in your muscles. Stand in second position. Feel your weight evenly over both legs.

2 Bend slowly and smoothly into your *demi-plié*. Keeping your heels on the floor, work your turnout as much as you can. For stability and control it is important to feel a line through the length of your spine. This is your centre of balance, or axis.

3 Bend your knees further, into a *grand plié*, and this time keep your heels on the floor throughout. Come up again as carefully as you went down. A *plié* should be beautifully balanced and smooth.

Battement tendu

THE WORD *battement* literally means "beat" or "beating". In ballet the word is used to define a whole family of movements where the working leg opens and closes. There are different kinds of *battement*, and each has its own value and character. When you perform them in class you will usually do one movement several times. At first you will practise them slowly, facing the barre. Then you will turn sideways to the barre. Finally you will practise them in the centre.

Battement tendu jeté
This exercise will help you to feel light and full of energy. *Jeté* means "thrown", but in *battement tendu jeté*, throw your leg only a few centimetres off the ground. Fix a point in the air with your toes before closing your legs.

Battement tendu
This exercise helps you to improve your turnout, warm up your legs, and get them strong and well prepared for the work ahead. *Tendu* means "stretched". You must feel the underneath of your foot stretch out along the floor.

Keep your head and shoulders poised and without strain.

Keep your back square.

Battement tendu derrière
Derrière means "behind". Slide your leg straight backwards from first or fifth position, leading with your toes.

Turn out your thigh as much as you can.

Battement tendu à la seconde
This is done to the side. Slide your leg out sideways trying to form a straight line through your stretched knee, instep, and toes.

Battement tendu devant
Devant means "in front". Lead with your heel and continue with your toes.

Keep your knee straight as you open your leg.

Keep your knee turned out.

Your supporting leg must work too. Try to keep it still, straight, and turned out. This will help the rest of your body to stay balanced.

When you have stretched out your leg fully, carefully close it again to the original position. Lower your whole foot gradually to the floor.

When your heel lifts off the floor, continue with your toes until you reach your maximum stretch.

Battement tendu soutenu

You will later find that the basic *battement tendu* can be developed in a wide variety of ways. In *soutenu*, your supporting leg makes a *demi-plié* as your stretched working leg slides out.

Feel the line from the top of your head to the tip of your toe.

This is a good exercise to improve your strength, flexibility, control, and coordination.

Keep your back very square and remember to hold your turnout.

It is important to keep your shoulders and hips level.

Advanced positions

When you are more advanced, you may finish your barre exercises, including *battement tendu* and *battement tendu jeté*, with a special pose or position. These varied shapes follow exact rules that you will learn step-by-step.

Try to feel graceful with a beautiful line through your neck and the top of your back to the tip of your toes.

Don't forget
It is important to feel confident at one level before you move on to the next.

Your supporting knee should be over your toes.

Rond de jambe

1 *Rond de jambe parterre* is a semi-circular movement made on the floor with your working leg. It will help you to feel the mobility of your hip joints. You can circle your leg either *en dehors* (outwards), or *en dedans* (inwards), as here. Slide your foot backwards as in *battement tendu*.

2 To begin with, move your arm and leg together. Then hold your arm in second position and continue to circle forwards with your leg. Turn your head to look straight forwards.

3 At first pause slightly in each position before moving on to the next. Keep your legs turned out and beautifully stretched.

4 Move your leg freely and smoothly so that your toes glide across the floor. Keep your supporting leg turned out and your tummy pulled up.

5 As you continue to circle your leg behind you again, it is important to keep your knee and foot stretched. You cannot look at it, so you must feel that it is correctly positioned.

6 During the *rond de jambe*, try to maintain your centre of balance, with your shoulders and hips level. As you circle your leg, your foot must be fully stretched with no weight resting on your working toes.

Battement fondu

YOU CAN LEARN many things from practising *battement fondu*, especially about how ballet and music work together. It is important to listen to the music while you are dancing, and your movements should reflect and express it. *Battement fondu* is a melting, flowing movement in which the legs work together smoothly, always with the music. Because *battement fondu* teaches you to work your legs with softness and elasticity, it will help you to join steps together in a velvety, seamless way. Later on, it will also help you to coordinate your jumps.

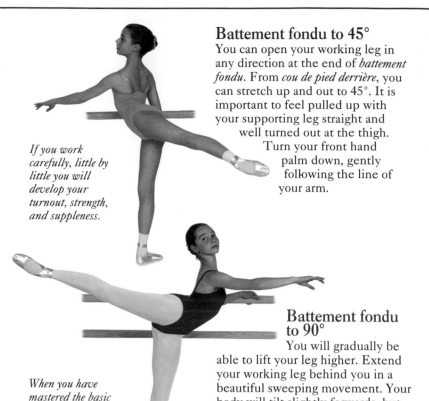

If you work carefully, little by little you will develop your turnout, strength, and suppleness.

Battement fondu to 45°
You can open your working leg in any direction at the end of *battement fondu*. From *cou de pied derrière*, you can stretch up and out to 45°. It is important to feel pulled up with your supporting leg straight and well turned out at the thigh. Turn your front hand palm down, gently following the line of your arm.

When you have mastered the basic fondu, *you may try* battement fondu *on* demi-pointe.

Battement fondu to 90°
You will gradually be able to lift your leg higher. Extend your working leg behind you in a beautiful sweeping movement. Your body will tilt slightly forwards, but hold the middle of your back strongly. Keep your neck gently curved and your front arm placed but light.

How to dance a battement fondu

At first you will learn *battement fondu* with your working toes on the floor, opening your leg to the side and then to the front and back. Your next step will be to open to 45° in each direction, with your supporting foot flat on the floor. After a lot of practice you will learn to rise to *demi-pointe* as you extend your working leg. Finally you will extend to 90° or more, rising to *demi-* or even full pointe. Advanced dancers will develop all these possibilities in fascinating and expressive ways.

Begin by looking at your fingertips.

Hold the barre lightly all the time. Don't grip with your hand: this will spoil your placing and posture and you will find it harder to work on your balance.

1 This is a *battement fondu* to second position to 45°. Start by standing in fifth, with your arm in preparatory position. During the musical introduction, take a breath to calm and prepare your whole body and mind for the movement.

Your hand should be soft and delicate.

2 Bring your arm carefully back through preparatory, following the movement with your eyes. At the same time, lift your working foot smoothly off the floor, keeping your heel well forwards, and begin to bend both knees together.

Wait until the moment that your toes leave the floor before gradually bending your knees.

Sur le cou de pied

This literally means "on the neck of the foot". In this position, your working foot is placed in a certain way on your other ankle. It can be flexed naturally, wrapped around, or fully stretched in *cou de pied*. The position forms the basis of many different steps. You can take it up smoothly, quickly, strongly, or lightly. Your supporting leg can be in a *demi-plié*, on a flat foot, or on *demi-pointe*.

Keep your heel forward.

With your knee and thigh turned out properly, this position is very useful for improving your turnout.

Devant
Here your supporting leg is in a *demi-plié* while your working foot is fully stretched in *cou de pied*. Place the tip of your toe exactly on your ankle bone.

Derrière
You can take up a *cou de pied* position with your supporting leg straight and your working foot placed *derrière*. Remember to hold the turnout of your working thigh.

Wrapped around
When placed *devant*, your working foot may be "wrapped around" your supporting ankle, with your heel towards the front and your toes behind.

Open your shoulders and keep them level with your hips.

As you open your leg sideways, look straight ahead.

Finish with your arm in second position.

Look gracefully into your hand.

Hold your arm precisely, but softly, in first position.

Remember to hold your turnout all the time.

3 As you *demi-plié* on one leg, show *cou de pied* exactly with the other, making sure your toe is very pointed. "Melt" to your deepest point and increase the turnout of both legs as much as you can. Your knees should look over your toes and your hips should stay level.

4 Open your working leg at the same time as you slowly stretch your supporting leg. Your legs must work together. Carry your free arm to second position. Keep the movement smooth and steady and stretch up through the length of your spine to feel light and lifted.

5 Your arm and leg must arrive in second position together. Stretch out as far as you can, while maintaining your centre of balance. It is important to keep well pulled up on your supporting side. If you direct your toes to an exact point in the air, you will capture a precise shape.

Don't forget
From start to finish, a *battement fondu* is always smooth and elastic, whatever the speed or rhythm of the music.

19

Further exercises

THE LANGUAGE of ballet is rich and varied. On stage you will have to change quickly from small, fast steps to smooth, graceful ones. You therefore need to get used to different ways and speeds of moving. The development and preparation in barrework exercises will help you. The exercises follow a logical pattern to make sure that, while gaining strength, you do not overwork your muscles. After the smooth elasticity of *battement fondu* you will be ready for some fast work close to the ground, such as *battement frappé* and *petit battement*. Following *rond de jambe en l'air*, you will be warm and ready for big movements to 90°. These can be slow and sustained, like *développé* and *relevé lent*, or fast and sweeping, like *grand battement*.

Petit battement

1 *Petit battement* means "small beat". This movement will help your lower leg to move quickly and freely. Your working foot can be pointed, flexed, or wrapped around in *cou de pied*.

2 Open your toes a little to the side, moving freely in the knee. Keep your thigh still and turned out.

3 Bring your working foot to *cou de pied derrière*. On the next beat, return your foot to the original position. Make your beats strong and accurate. Your teacher will tell you how many to do.

Battement frappé

1 *Frapper* means "to strike". This movement is fast and energetic. It will help to develop strength and flexibility in your lower leg. Your working foot can be pointed, flexed, or wrapped around in *cou de pied*.

2 Open your lower leg quickly and strongly to second position, keeping your thigh turned out and still. At first put an equal accent on opening and closing. Later you will extend to a position just off the floor and accent the opening more, as if "striking" the air.

Développé

Place your hand correctly on the barre.

1 *Battement développé* is a big unfolding movement of *adage*. It helps to make you strong and supple. You can unfold in any direction, but at first you will do it slowly, to learn balance and control. For *développé à la seconde*, start in fifth with your working arm in preparatory position.

Don't let this arm move.

2 Breathe and gently open the lower part of your arm sideways from preparatory position, starting with your fingertips. Look elegantly at your hand as it opens. Bring your arm back through preparatory position as the exercise begins.

3 Holding your turnout as you move, lift your working leg through *cou de pied*. Make sure your toes and instep are stretched and your heel is well forward. Lift your arm to first position.

4 Slide your toe up to *retiré* position. Take it right up to your knee and keep increasing your turnout as you go. The unfolding should be clear and light, not dull and heavy. Try not to let this look difficult.

Keep your supporting leg taut and your body lifted.

5 Extend your leg smoothly and freely to 90° and open your arm to second position. Keep your back square and your shoulders open and level. Hold your leg very still in the open position, then lower slowly and carefully to fifth position.

Work hard to make each pose correct, expressive, and artistic.

Even when you lift your leg high, keep your shoulders level.

Let the movement "speak". This shape has a soft flying line.

In time, your adage movements, and the ways you join them together, will become more complicated and varied.

Attitude *effacée derrière*

Arabesque *penchée*

Second arabesque *en fondu*

Do not roll your supporting foot.

Adage

The word *adage* comes from the musical term for a slow tempo. In ballet too, *adage* is slow and graceful. To begin with you will study each new shape slowly and carefully so that you have plenty of time to hold it and balance calmly and freely. Ultimately you will learn all the poses of classical ballet, including attitudes and arabesques.

Hold your arm still and perfectly placed in second position.

More expression

Slowly, but surely, from your first simple exercises of *développé* and *relevé lent*, your *adage* will grow in meaning and expressiveness, engaging your heart and soul.

Lift your leg only as high as you can while keeping your correct placing and turnout. As you get stronger, you will be able to lift to 90° and higher.

For strength and lightness

This big movement can be done quickly as *grand battement jeté*, when you throw your leg up, or slowly as *relevé lent,* when you lift your leg slowly. It is important to learn both, as they are strengthening in different ways. *Relevé lent* will help you to hold your leg still and well placed at its maximum height. *Grand battement* is more active and energetic. It will help you to become flexible and supple. Both movements will help to give your legs the lightness and extension, or height, needed for classical ballet.

You can lift your leg to the front, to the side, or to the back.

Be patient
Build up your technique step-by-step.

When you lower your leg, bring it down with control until your toe touches the floor, then close.

Keep your supporting leg well stretched and turned out.

Bending

B ALLET IS AN ART that will make extreme demands on your body. To be a dancer you must be supple, strong, and well coordinated. You need to be able to jump and have turned out legs that can lift up lightly and easily. With the ever increasing physical demands, special exercises will play an important supporting role in your training. But remember that ballet is first and foremost an art. So when you do bending or other special exercises, try to imagine how they will help you with the balletic movements you are also learning.

Learning to lift
This exercise will help you to feel the muscles in your bottom and the back of your thighs. It will strengthen your back too. When you are lying on the floor, it is easier to feel if you are straining your shoulders or twisting your hips as you lift your leg behind you. Carefully correct your mistakes now, to be ready for arabesques.

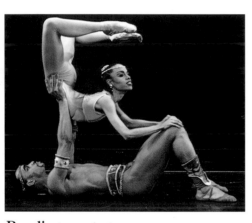

Bending on stage
Some ballets require more flexibility than others! This is a pose from the ballet *Medea*, performed by the Dance Theatre of Harlem.

Your head and hands should always complete the picture. Place them correctly and elegantly as you stretch sideways, and keep your head and body in perfect alignment.

Stretching in a sitting position
There are many stretching exercises you can do sitting down. These will help you to develop the right sort of suppleness, and to pinpoint areas that might be a little stiff. When you bend sideways, you are stretching the muscles on the side you lean away from. You should be able to feel a gentle, painless stretch.

When you are sitting down, your legs do not have to support your weight. You will therefore find it easier to concentrate on your back, neck, and arms.

Be careful
There is a big difference between sustained effort and force! Don't force your body into shapes it does not want to make.

Professional dancers have their own special sequences of warming up exercises before class begins. Your teacher will help you to work out exercises for your feet, tummy, and back muscles.

Limbering up

As a professional dancer, I rehearse every day and perform on many evenings too. I have to be light on my feet and sometimes have to move very fast. My body must be perfectly tuned to withstand this work, and I am therefore careful to keep it flexible by limbering up properly.

Keep breathing

Breathe naturally with the movement of each exercise. Rhythmical breathing helps with the flow of movement and therefore with its range and suppleness.

The splits

You should do limbering up exercises like the splits only after your barrework or at the end of the class. Your muscles must be very warm or you will strain them. Getting flexible enough to do the splits may take several months or more of practice, and some people never manage it. Don't twist your hips or force your body awkwardly.

Bending forwards

In class you will practise bending forwards and backwards with balletic arm movements. Bend forwards gradually and smoothly, keeping your legs taut and turned out. Lower your arm naturally as you bend, and try hard not to sway backwards from your hips.

Bending backwards

Hold your arm in a curve above your head. Hold your back well and your tummy muscles strongly. Start to go back, shoulders and upper back first. You can go back only a little way with just the top of your back, then your lower back will take over the movement.

Going further

Be careful to control the line of your head and arm as you go further back. You should keep them in the same position. Bend as far as you can without forcing, and don't let your hips push forwards. Breathe out as you bend back. Breathe in to help you return to the upright position.

Using all your muscles

Your exercises have to be well balanced. Don't overwork one group of muscles at the expense of others. After stretching sideways, you should bend backwards and forwards. Keep both hands on your knees.

Always feel the length and balance of your spine before you move.

Extend and lengthen your spine as you bend back. Feel as if the front of your ribcage was lifting up from within.

Curl your head down towards your knees, starting with the top of your neck and continuing down to the bottom of your back. When you come up, reverse the movement, uncurling from the base of your back first.

Using your arms

A VITAL PART of the art of dancing is the way dancers use their arms. This is called *port de bras*, which literally means "carriage of the arms". Although you learn arm movements separately, you should not think of them in isolation. Your arms should work harmoniously with the movements of your whole body. At first the forms are simple. Later, when you have learned to combine it with bends and turns of the body, *port de bras* will be involved in everything you do. Different schools have their own particular patterns and sequences for teaching *port de bras*, but all aim at the same goals of finesse, harmony, and expression.

How to hold your hands

Basic hand position
Place your hand so that it looks natural and relaxed. Keep your fingers delicately and softly grouped.

Allongé
This position is a nuance and a refinement of the basic position. Open your fingers and gently turn your palm downwards.

Advanced port de bras

You will need supervision
You will not learn this sort of *port de bras* until you are advanced, and only with the guidance of your teacher.

Listen very carefully to the music and breathe naturally, feeling the rise and fall of each movement.

Lift your eyes and then watch your hand.

1 This is an advanced *port de bras* sequence, because it involves bending your body forwards, sideways, and backwards, as well as using your arms. Start in fifth position, *épaulement croisé*, with your arms in preparatory position. During the musical introduction, take your arms up, passing through first position.

2 Lift up and over as you bend forwards smoothly.

3 Continue bending forwards. Lower your head and bring your hands together. Try to let the movements flow smoothly and without tension.

4 Begin to come up smoothly and naturally. Keep your hands placed and look at them. Hold your shoulders down and your hips still.

Keep your legs stretched and in a tight fifth position. Don't sway backwards.

Simple port de bras

When you have learned the rules for the placing and posture of your arms, you are ready to start joining the shapes together. For this simple *port de bras* exercise, start in preparatory position, then prepare your arms, passing through first position. Let your head and eyes follow the smooth, free movement of your arms.

Keep your shoulders open and lowered.

Try to keep your body lifted and poised.

Arms used choreographically

On stage you will use your arms to help you portray a wonderful range of characters and feelings. The exact movements will be determined by the choreographer of the ballet. Here the Houston Ballet from the United States is performing *Serenade,* choreographed by George Balanchine.

Be guided by the music and feel its life within you as you move.

All the time your body is bending, keep your legs strong and straight, and do not roll your feet.

5 Bring your body up until you are standing upright again. Your arms should be elegantly curved in front of you in first position.

6 Still looking into your hands, turn slightly away from the audience. Keep your shoulders level and open, and your hips still.

7 Raise your right arm and open your left as you start to bend smoothly backwards. Follow your top arm around with your head and eyes, naturally and easily.

8 Bring your body upright as you gracefully change your arms to return to your starting position.

Classical ballet poses

THE BASIC POSES in classical ballet have been developed over centuries and form the structure on which the whole of ballet rests. There is a great variety of ways in which poses can be developed and performed, but, underneath the elaboration, the basic shapes are always recognizable. This is why it is important to learn them correctly from the beginning. Perform them with feeling and, above all, remember to involve your whole body, from your head and eyes to your toes and fingertips.

On stage
When you perform on stage, you will have to project your work differently according to your size and shape. Here, three dancers from The Royal Ballet take up a pose, *croisé devant* with both arms up, during the ballet *The Nutcracker*.

Ecarté devant
This pose has a very noble feeling. It is set on the diagonal with your leg, arms, and head all on the same plane. Stand as if you were facing a corner of the front of the stage. Extend the leg nearest the audience to second position. Hold your downstage arm up and your other arm to the side. Keep your hips level and incline your body slightly away from the audience.

You incline your body differently in each pose. This is an important part of its feeling and character.

Croisé devant
This *croisé* pose is bright and clear. You usually learn *croisé* positions and poses first. For *croisé devant*, stretch the leg nearer the audience in front of you. Hold your upstage arm high and your other arm to the side. Look out to the audience and incline the top of your body slightly back.

Ecarté derrière
This pose has a softer, giving feeling. This time extend the leg further from the audience to second position. Hold your upstage arm up and your other arm to the side. Incline your body and head slightly towards the audience and look down, along the line of your arm. Your head should be in profile.

The meanings
Ecarté means "separated"; *croisé* means "crossed"; *effacé* usually means "open" in ballet. Take these words and translate them into movement.

Keep your legs beautifully stretched.

In this pose, the line of your head crosses the line of your leg. To the audience, your whole body appears crossed.

Attitudes

There is a special pose in ballet called an attitude. It is a position on one leg, with the other leg lifted and bent either behind or in front of you. You will find that you use attitudes more in advanced work, in *adage*, and in jumps, turns, and lifts. When you are young, you will learn it slowly and carefully, either *croisé* or *effacé*, with the basic arm positions.

There is a delicate quality to the line of your head and neck.

Both of these attitudes are being danced croisé.

Keep your shoulders level. At 90° incline forwards very slightly.

Correct alignment

This diagram will help you to visualize the particular direction of a movement and the amount of turn your body has to make for épaulement *croisé or* effacé.

This position is effacé devant parterre.

Upstage (the back of the stage)

Downstage (the front of the stage)

To help you to visualize the different positions of the body when you are learning, imagine that you are standing in the middle of a "star" of lines. You can then make sure your body is aligned correctly for *épaulement croisé* or *effacé*, or the *écarté* lines.

Place your arms exactly. Let your head and eyes complete the shape and don't forget to breathe in harmony with the movements.

Effacé devant

In *effacé* poses, the line of your body is open to the audience. For *effacé devant*, extend the leg further from the audience in front of you. Hold your downstage arm high and your other arm to the side. Lean your body slightly back, with your top arm gently framing your face. Look clearly up and out.

Effacé poses should have an elusive flying quality.

Use your whole body

The way you look must reflect the feeling of the pose. Concentrate the whole of your body into discovering its meaning. Give "spirit" to your pose by using your eyes to express the feeling.

Croisé derrière

This pose has a strong direct feeling. Extend the leg further from the audience behind you. Hold the same arm high and your other arm out to the side. Turn your head towards the audience. Keep your body straight.

Make sure that your extended leg is exactly in front of or behind you, following the rules for battement tendu.

Effacé derrière

This pose has a wistful quality. Stretch your downstage leg behind you. Hold the arm on the same side high and your other arm out to the side. Lean slightly forwards, lift your face and eyes a little, and imagine you are flying.

Arabesques

ONE OF THE MOST BEAUTIFUL poses in ballet is the arabesque. The word originally described a form of ancient ornamental design, which used the flowing lines of branches, leaves, and scrolls. These were fancifully intertwined in complicated, yet beautifully balanced, patterns. In ballet too, the dancer must be perfectly balanced, standing on one leg with the other well stretched out behind. The arms are extended in harmony with the legs, and the dancer forms a graceful curve from fingertips to toes.

Keep this leg beautifully stretched and turned out with a fully arched foot.

Develop a basic shape
There are many different arabesques. You will learn the basic shapes first. Later you will find that each one can be developed in a huge variety of ways to convey many different feelings and moods.

Try to visualize the shape you want to make with your leg, and feel the line exactly.

Keep your shoulders lowered and open.

Your gaze should be steady and following the line of your arm.

Hold your arms softly stretched.

Learning arabesques
To start with you will learn an arabesque *parterre* to find the correct placing of your arms, legs, and body. The toes of your extended leg stay on the ground. Make sure there is no weight resting on them. Keep your body well lifted and try not to lean forwards. To perform the arabesque shown here, stand on your right leg, open your left arm forwards and your right arm to the side. This is called an arabesque *croisée* because your legs appear crossed to the audience.

Arabesque to 90°
As you get stronger, you will be able to lift your leg higher. Try not to lean away from your centre of balance as your leg goes up. Let your pelvis tilt forwards slightly, but keep your tummy lifted so you don't lose the lovely curved line. Try to find the perfect shape and balance. Remember what it feels like so that you can find it again next time.

Hold your hands palm down and softly stretched, with your fingertips leading the way.

Do not let your thumb drop too much and spoil the flowing line.

More than just a step

As you progress, you will learn to use your head and eyes to make your arabesques even more artistic. Many dancers can perform the basic step, but only some can convey a special feeling and intensity. This is Miyako Yoshida performing a beautiful arabesque *penchée*. She is dancing with Petter Jacobsson for The Birmingham Royal Ballet in *Theme and Variations*.

Be careful not to drop your elbows.

Placing your whole body

Whichever style of arabesque you are peforming, try to feel the placing of the whole of your body. Keep your back strong and square and your working leg stretched and turned out. Turn both hands palm down and hold them softly. Your head should be poised, with your eyes following the line of your arm. The turning of your palms and stretching out of your arms should convey a feeling of flight to the audience.

When you start to study arabesques, hold your side arm slightly in front of your shoulder line. As you get older, your teacher will ask you gradually to open your side arm at the shoulder joint.

Feel a perfect line softly flowing from fingertips to fingertips through your arms, back, and shoulders.

As you get stronger, try to keep the shoulder of your supporting side well lowered, and slightly drawn back.

Keep your supporting leg well turned out and as straight as possible.

Advanced arabesques

After years of practice you will try more difficult arabesques, such as this one. With the same arm forwards as your raised leg, turn your head to look over your front shoulder. Your back should be more strongly arched than in some other arabesques, and the whole feeling should be more upright. This pose gives the impression that you are soaring upwards like a bird.

It is important to keep the correct placing of your legs. Hold your hips level. Do not tip them towards the audience.

Croisé parterre

This arabesque is particularly expressive in the beautiful sweep of line through your back and neck as you turn your shoulders. Try to feel the line through the curve of your neck and down through the centre of your body as your arms and shoulders move.

Linking movements

BALLET DOES not consist only of positions. It is a dance in which the positions are joined by special movements. You will practise every classical ballet step individually until it is good enough to put together with others. The linking movements are as important as the positions they join. You should work hard to understand the technique, rhythm, and timing of your linking steps. Then you will be able to develop the phrasing of your dancing to give it light and shade, colour, and vibrancy. On stage you will want to accent some steps more than others. For this, a good understanding of your linking steps is essential.

Follow the movement of your hand with your eyes.

Don't forget
All exercises should be practised to the right and to the left. Travelling steps should be practised going backwards, too.

It is a lovely feeling to skim swiftly across the floor with tiny little steps. Keep to a definite line. With practice, you will feel as if you were floating across the room.

Pas couru

This is a run in any direction, and is a very useful joining step. *Pas couru* can be danced as a preparation for jumps. It can join different types of step together and make it easy for you to change direction. It can also be a little run in first position with your feet facing forward instead of turned out.

1 You can start *pas couru* from various positions, sometimes with a *pas dégagé*, that is, with your foot pointed in an open position. Make a *battement tendu effacé devant* with a demi-plié.

Hold your arms as if they were resting on a beautiful full skirt.

2 Transfer your weight to your opening leg very smoothly, and glide into a run.

Your hands can be high or low. Plan what you are going to do, then feel as delicate and free as a bird.

3 Take tiny steps travelling forwards. Imagine that you are gently pushing your skirt away from you, or that you are gliding through a soft mist.

Temps lié

One of the most important linking movements is *temps lié*. You will use it to transfer smoothly from one position to another. Danced in the centre, it is an exercise complete in itself. It helps you to develop the coordination of your whole body and your feeling for dance. Perform it as if you were pouring one movement into the other. *Temps lié* can become a more complicated exercise with bends of the body, high legs, and turns, and there may be slight differences of timing and style.

Try to get the details of each shape correct.

1 *Temps lié en avant* travels forwards. Start in fifth position with *épaulement croisé* and your arms low.

Incline your head to look into your hands.

2 Take a small breath to free your arms, then *demi-plié*. Look into your hands.

3 Keep your back leg in *demi-plié* and stretch your other leg forwards with a gliding feeling. Raise your arms in front of you to first position.

Keep your body precisely placed and balanced.

4 With your weight on your back foot, continue to stretch your pointed toe forwards, still on the floor. Transfer your weight very smoothly to your front foot to the pose *croisé derrière*.

5 Close your back foot into fifth position *croisé*, turn *en face*, and *demi-plié*. Lower your top arm to first position, watching your hand as it moves.

6 Keep your back leg in *demi-plié* and stretch your other one to the side. Open your arm.

Hold your turnout as you transfer your weight.

7 Stretch your pointed toe along the floor, then transfer your weight immediately, but smoothly. Point the other foot to second position, still facing the front, and *allongé* your hands.

Follow your hand with your eyes.

8 Close your legs with the music to fifth position *épaulement croisé*. Close your arms to preparatory position and look out to the audience.

Pas de bourrée

Practising *pas de bourrée* will help you to achieve neat and lively footwork. There are many forms of *pas de bourrée*, usually involving three quick changes of weight. You will learn them facing the barre and later, when you can perform them accurately, you will bring them into the centre. The extraordinary versatility of *pas de bourrée* means it can join many different types of step together.

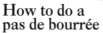

4 Finish this *pas couru* in a position that flows naturally and artistically from the movement.

How to do a pas de bourrée

Start in *demi-plié* with your foot in *cou de pied derrière*. Gather yourself up quickly and lightly, and replace one foot with the other. Bring your arms to first position. Change feet again with a tiny step, lightly and exactly. Finish in *cou de pied derrière* in a *demi-plié* with *épaulement croisé*.

As you change your weight in pas de bourrée, you never have two feet on the ground at the same time.

Pirouettes

IN CLASSICAL BALLET there are many different ways of turning. As you advance, you will find that almost every movement can be danced *en tournant*, or going round. A pirouette is a special and exciting step in ballet when you spin round on one leg. To prepare you for pirouettes, you will do simple exercises at the barre and in the centre, on two feet. These will help you to get the right strength, control, and energy. You will learn your first pirouettes with your raised leg in either *cou de pied* or *retiré* position. Later you can extend your leg into any one of the big poses you have studied. These are called *grandes* pirouettes.

Spotting for a pirouette
When you start to turn your body in a pirouette, delay the turn of your head a little. Fix your eyes on something, keeping your chin level. Then quickly bring your head round. Your body will follow. If you do this properly, it can help you not to get dizzy.

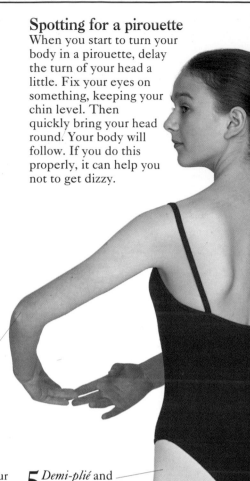

Do not let your elbows drop.

How to do a pirouette

1 Pirouettes turn *en dehors* and *en dedans*, and it is important to practise them both ways. The basic pirouettes are from fourth, fifth, or second position. This is a preparation followed by a pirouette from fourth position *en dehors*. Stand in fifth *croisé*, your arms in preparatory, and your head turned to look over your front shoulder.

2 *Demi-plié*, lift your arms slightly, and look into your hands.

3 Spring into *retiré* position, your arms in first, to face the other corner. Find your centre of balance, or axis, and hold it strongly.

4 Lower your raised leg to fourth position *croisé*. Open your arms with your hands *allongées*.

5 *Demi-plié* and push up into *retiré* position. Hold your arms in first and turn your body and legs exactly together in one fixed shape.

Hold your arms steady, but not stiffly.

Don't let the heel of your supporting leg slip and turn in as you push up.

32

Keep your eyes level as you move your head.

Your head will come quickly round to the front in advance of your body.

Stay vertical throughout this type of pirouette. Hold your shoulders level and your hips square, and keep your body still.

6 Complete the pirouette firmly and calmly in a *demi-plié*. The finish is as important as the start. If you fall at the end of a turn, the audience will know that you are out of control.

Hold your back strongly, especially at the waist.

Hold your toe exactly in place as you turn.

Keep your supporting leg taut and both legs turned out throughout the pirouette.

Make sure that your knees are looking over your toes as you close to fifth position, and do not roll forwards.

Preparing for pirouettes

Don't try to turn before you can balance. Before you learn a proper pirouette, you can practise doing lots of *relevé* preparations without a turn. This simple preparatory exercise will help you to feel the correct line and balance of your body. It will also help you to keep your body still and your legs taut and turned out.

1 Stand *en face* in fifth position with one arm in front and the other to the side. *Demi-plié*, remembering to keep your feet placed evenly on the floor.

Keep your shoulders open and level.

2 *Relevé* strongly but calmly to *retiré* position. Feel your centre line of balance, and pull your body up through it to feel tall and thin.

3 Close your leg neatly behind to fifth position in a *demi-plié* with *épaulement croisé*. Feel composed when you finish, with your weight evenly on both feet.

33

First jumps

JUMPS ARE an important and exciting part of your class. Everything that you have worked on up to now has been preparing you for this moment. You can jump at different heights and speeds. You can stay on the spot or travel. At first, boys and girls learn the same jumping steps. As boys grow and develop more muscle, their steps become more complicated. They need to be strong and powerful as they jump. Girls will work for lightness, grace, and delicacy. In music, the word *allegro* means brisk and lively. This describes the quality needed for jumps in ballet. You will start with *petit allegro*. These are small neat steps. Later, when you become stronger, you will be able to jump higher. This is called *grand allegro*.

Preparation for a jump

Your preparation before a jump is important. It must be clear, rhythmical, and exact. In the *demi-plié* before you spring up, press your whole foot, especially your heels, into the floor. This will give you the strength to push up into the air.

In the air

Be sure about what shape you are trying to make in the air. Fix your position exactly and stretch your legs and feet as much as you can. Remember to finish calmly and correctly.

Understand the exercises
To help you have lovely stretched feet in the air, you must make sure that you understand the exercises you do for your feet and insteps at the start of class.

Temps levé

The first and simplest jump you will learn is a *temps levé*. It is a jump on the spot, beginning and ending on two legs in a *demi-plié*. It can be done in any of the five positions of the feet. Later you will do a *temps levé* from one leg.

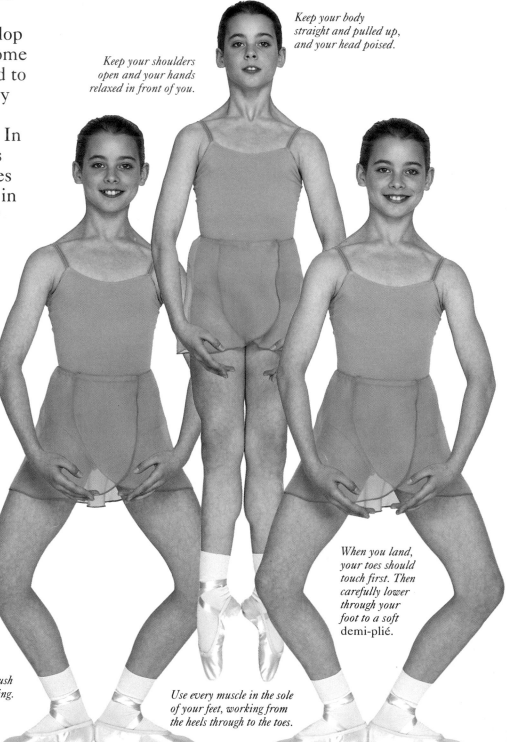

Keep your shoulders open and your hands relaxed in front of you.

Keep your body straight and pulled up, and your head poised.

When you land, your toes should touch first. Then carefully lower through your foot to a soft demi-plié.

Hold your turnout and push from your heels like a spring.

Use every muscle in the sole of your feet, working from the heels through to the toes.

Pas échappé sauté

1 *Echapper* means to escape, and an *échappée sautée* is a jump in which your legs open or "escape" from one another to a different position. You can do a *petite échappée* or a *grande échappée*. Start in fifth position, then go into a *demi-plié*, ready to spring into the air. In *grande échappée* you will need to go into a deeper *demi-plié* for more power.

2 This is where *petite* and *grande échappée* differ most. In *petite échappée*, open your legs directly to second position in the air. In *grande échappée*, as you jump up, keep your feet together in a tight fifth position.

3 In *petite échappée*, land after opening your legs to second. For *grande échappée*, open your legs to second position only at the moment of your return to the floor. Keep your *demi-plié* very even with the whole of each foot on the floor.

4 Without releasing your muscles, push strongly off the floor. Fix second position in the air, keeping your legs taut and your toes stretched. Try to increase your turnout. Keep your arms light but properly placed – simple and low for *petite échappée*; higher and wider for *grande échappée*.

5 Land again in fifth position in a soft but steady and elastic *demi-plié*. Stretch your legs to finish. With more experience, you may do an *échappée* to fourth position, *croisé* or *effacé*. Your teacher may also ask you to finish on one leg instead of two.

Petite échappée

Grande échappée

Move correctly
It is important to be very correct and clear as you move from one position to the next.

Petite *means small, and this jump is a low one.*

Grande *means big. This jump is higher.*

Hold your turnout.

The need for strong muscles

Dancing the role of the frog Mr. Jeremy Fisher in *Tales of Beatrix Potter* involves a lot of jumping. Here, William Trevitt seems to hover in the air as he jumps from lily pad to lily pad. A jump like this needs strength and elasticity in the muscles and ligaments of the legs and feet. Careful preparation helps to get good jumps. If your muscles work properly at the beginning of your training, your dancing will look poised and fluent when you grow up.

Sissonne simple

This is a jump from two legs to one. *Demi-plié* in fifth position and push off the floor using your heels, insteps, and toes. Bring your head straight and use your arms to help you. Feel as if your whole body is gathered up into the air. Land on one leg, the other neatly in *cou de pied*.

Do not roll over on your big or little toes.

Keep the whole of your foot on the floor.

Bigger jumps

WHEN your muscles have developed strength and resilience in simple jumps, you can attempt the larger jumps of *grand allegro*. These jumps are exciting, but also very demanding. You must be thoroughly prepared and warm before attempting them. In ballet, the way you enter a jump, the way you hold it in the air, and the way you complete it must all be artistic and precise. Enthusiasm, intelligence, and sensitivity will help you to transform the merely physical and gymnastic into art.

As in all sissonnes, *make sure that your head is moving in harmony with your arms and body.*

Jumping balletically

There are many kinds of jump. They can bounce, skim across the floor, or soar into the air. Each jump has its own look and feel, giving a variety of possibilities to choreographers. Here, Miyako Yoshida of The Birmingham Royal Ballet is performing a *grand jeté* in attitude from Ashton's ballet *La Fille mal Gardée.*

Sissonne fondue

This is a jump from the *sissonne* family. *Sissonnes* can be large or small, landing on one leg, or closing quickly. They can be swift and neat, or they can soar into the air. You can even beat or turn them. *Sissonnes* start from two feet and have a flying quality, whatever the speed, height, and direction. After landing in *sissonne fondue*, close your raised leg smoothly to fifth position. Your final *demi-plié* should be soft and melting.

Prepare carefully

It is important that the preparations that lead you into a jump are correct rhythmically and physically. Then you will get the proper impetus off the ground and shape in the air.

Ballonné

At first you will learn this jump *sur place*, or on the spot. Later you will learn to travel, flying forwards, backwards, or sideways, doing one *ballonné* after another. *Ballonné* should be rhythmical and staccato – like bouncing. It needs beautiful coordination, and the position of your arms and head must be exact.

1 This is a *ballonné* to the side in second position. Start in fifth position with *épaulement croisé.*

2 *Demi-plié* as you slide your foot out, and push powerfully and energetically up off the floor.

In ballonnés *you fly through the air in the direction of your opening leg.*

3 Throw your leg strongly and cleanly to second position in the air, keeping a vertical line through your body.

Once in the air, stretch your legs, hold the shape, and then return safely to the ground.

On stage

Fiona Chadwick and Jonathan Cope, both performing a *grand jeté* in *La Bayadère*, show an exciting part of advanced *grand allegro*. *Grand allegro* can be developed in many ways in the progression from class to the stage.

Ballon

Appearing to hover at the high point of certain jumps is called *ballon*.

Pas de chat

This movement imitates the jump of a cat. (*Pas de chat* means "step of the cat".) There are several different forms of *pas de chat*, and they all need exact coordination of the body, arms, and legs. For this version, prepare your arms and then *demi-plié* in fifth position. Quickly lift your back foot to *cou de pied derrière*, then spring lightly upwards and forwards into the air, arms in front of you. At the end of the jump, close into a *demi-plié* in fifth position, with your arms and head completing the picture.

Bring this leg through quickly and lightly.

Keep your shoulders and thighs level, and fix the shape in the air.

Don't sit in your demi-pliés. Spring quickly into the air to show the position straight away.

Precise and sensitive footwork is essential for good elevation.

4 Land in a *demi-plié*, simultaneously closing your raised leg to *cou de pied devant*.

5 Spring quickly off the ground again to exactly the same position in the air.

6 Finish the second *ballonné* in *cou de pied derrière*. Be careful to land absolutely on balance.

On your toes

BALLERINAS first danced on the tip of their toes at the beginning of the 19th century. It made them appear weightless and fragile, and became an important and admired quality of the Romantic ballets of the 1830s and 40s. Good pointework looks effortless and expressive, but it is actually the result of very hard work. You should not attempt to dance on pointe until your feet and legs are sufficiently strong. This will probably be when you are about 11 years old, and when you have already trained carefully for several years.

For relevé in fifth position, keep your legs taut, turned out, and very close together.

Tie your ribbons neatly – tight enough to support you, but loose enough to leave your ankle free to move.

Rosin is made from the sap of fir trees. It crumbles into a white powder if you step on it.

Preparing to dance
After tying your shoes, put the tip of your toes into the rosin box, one foot at a time. A little rosin on your shoes will help you to avoid slipping on a wooden floor. It should not be necessary on a vinyl floor, which is not so slippery.

Perfect positioning
It is a wonderful feeling when you dance on the tip of your toes. You feel light and delicate. But do not try to dance on pointe until your body, legs, and feet are strong enough to lift you up and carefully bring you down again. Try to keep a vertical line through the centre of your feet. It is especially important not to allow your feet to sickle when on pointe. Sickling is when you let your instep fall inwards or outwards, which can lead to injury.

Make sure the drawstrings in your shoes are comfortably pulled up and tucked in.

Relevés

1 You will start to dance on pointe with simple exercises facing the barre to gain strength and stability. To do this *relevé*, start in first position.

2 Move smoothly into a *demi-plié*, making sure your heels are pressed firmly into the floor. Holding your turnout, push strongly up on to pointe. Lower carefully back into a *demi-plié*.

Pas échappé

1 *Demi-plié* in fifth position, then spring lightly on to pointe in second. Skim your toes along the floor to "escape" from the *demi-plié*.

2 Keeping lifted and light, close your legs simultaneously back to *demi-plié* in fifth position.

Keep your back straight and poised.

Keep your knees and insteps stretched and still, with your weight evenly balanced over both feet.

Pas glissade

This gliding movement is one of the steps you will learn when you have gained enough strength and confidence to dance on pointe in the centre of the room.

Your head should complete each shape and movement. Your gaze should be focused, yet free.

You can hold up either arm for this pose.

Concentrate on your legs and feet, but remember about your arms. Try to make each movement a complete picture in which your whole body is in harmony.

Always sew your own ribbons into your shoes so that you get the fit exactly right.

1 Start with a *demi-plié* in fifth position and stretch your leg forwards with a sliding movement. Lift your arms slightly and look gracefully into your hands.

2 Transfer your weight forwards to your front pointe exactly on the spot shown by your toes. Close your back foot tightly behind to a really exact fifth position on pointe.

Pointe shoes

The tip of pointe shoes is made of layers of satin, paper, and a coarse material called burlap, glued together. New shoes feel stiff and hard and there is no left and right. Take time and care to work them in to make them pliable and shaped to your feet. You need to feel as one with your shoes, as if they were a second skin. Then you will be able to "speak with your feet".

Advanced pointework

Y OUR CLASSES and exercises will give you the basic strength you need to progress in pointework. But physical ability alone is not enough. You need many different qualities, such as poise, suppleness, strength, and lightness. These all need to be developed in harmony. Don't over-emphasize one and forget about the others. Although you need strength for dancing on pointe, remember that it is essentially very graceful and feminine.

Relevé croisé derrière
As you progress, your work will become more intricate and artistic. Finally you will be ready to move from the classroom to the stage.

Elite Syncopations
Here, Zoltan Solymosi and I are dancing in Kenneth MacMillan's ballet *Elite Syncopations*. The ballet is set to ragtime music by several composers, including Scott Joplin.

Perfect pointe
You must resist the temptation to rely on your shoes to hold you up on pointe. It will not only make your work look dull and heavy, but will wear your shoes out much faster. Use your muscles instead. Try to balance perfectly on the tip of your toe. Your foot should look so strong and poised that the audience believes you could stand on pointe without a shoe. I am dancing here in *Elite Syncopations*.

Pointework technique

Sometimes you will want to move smoothly, holding each movement so that it melts into the next. For this you must lower delicately from the tip of your toes. At other times you will want to move quickly. Your footwork must then be staccato, neat, and exciting.

Relevé attitude *croisée devant*

The costumes for Elite Syncopations *were designed by Ian Spurling. MacMillan wanted this dance in the ballet to look chic, yet refined.*

Attitude *croisée derrière*

Let your head and arms complement the line of your legs. The complete picture should be balanced and tasteful.

Make sure that your supporting knee is completely stretched at the top of the movement. Capture the shape.

While your legs are working hard, your body should maintain an easy gracefulness.

Stretched knees, taut leg muscles, and strong feet and ankles all help with stability on pointe.

Think about what you are doing
With each step you do, have a clear idea of the different effects you are trying to achieve.

Pas ballonné

You can travel forwards, backwards, or sideways with this step, and you can use *épaulement croisé* or *effacé*. Travel as you *relevé*, then lower down on the spot. At first hold your arms in a simple position. Later you can change your *port de bras* to suit the vituosity of this step.

As you spring forwards on to pointe, throw your working leg out in front of you to 45°.

This ballonné *is travelling* effacé *en avant.*

Keep your back strong, especially as you lower into your demi-plié.

41

Pas de deux

AT THE BEGINNING of the 19th century, the difference between the steps for men and the steps for women became much more obvious. Women moved lightly and gracefully, and began to dance on the tip of their toes, while men emphasized strength and nobility in their movements. The men began to lift and support the women and sweep them up. So began the wonderful world of *pas de deux*. A *pas de deux* is, above all, a partnership between two dancers, physically, musically, and artistically. It is wonderfully exciting to dance when everything you do depends on your rapport with your partner, and when you inspire each other to greater heights.

Learning together

In *pas de deux* it is important that partners match each other physically. The girl should be smaller and lighter than the boy, but strong enough to dance the required steps. You will first learn correct placing through supported *adage*, when you work together without lifting. Practise feeling your own central line of balance and its relationship to your work with your partner.

Dance in harmony

You must try to keep each part of your own body dancing in harmony, while also coordinating your movements with your partner. You must both learn to breathe and balance together. The girl should respond and react. The boy should feel the rhythm and movement of the girl when supporting, holding, or lifting her so that she can keep her balance.

Enchaînement

There are rules for every shape and movement you make together. With practice, you will understand enough to link steps together in simple choreographed sequences. These are called *enchaînements*.

The movement of your head is very important. It should move correctly and easily to any position.

The boy needs to support the girl confidently, but not be tense or rigid.

You must listen and respond to the music together.

The girl should not change her position until each particular movement is completed.

1 To work on and perform this *enchaînement*, prepare together to pointe *tendue croisée derrière* with your arms in second position. Look out to the audience.

2 Let your heads lead the movement into a small waltz step. Make sure you are both moving together physically and musically, and that the balance of movement between you is artistic.

3 Now both change direction. The girl steps forwards to first arabesque on pointe. The boy must be ready to judge how far away he must stand for the girl to keep her balance. He stands behind her with the palm of his hands placed firmly on the sides of her waist with his first fingers and thumbs curved around it.

N

Start simply
When you begin *pas de deux* work, it is important that you do not do things that are too complicated or physically demanding. It will take time for you to feel each other's balance and coordinate movements.

Practice is important
Lifts require precise timing and coordination from both partners. I always practise with my partner, in this case Zoltan Solymosi, until we both know exactly what the other is going to do. Then we can feel, adjust, and prepare for a performance. I always remember that a great deal depends on how I start and finish each movement. This lift is from a *pas de deux* in the ballet *Swan Lake*.

Concentrate on complementing each other in line and movement.

4 Using his hands, the boy brings the girl's body upright as she closes her raised leg to fifth position. When he feels she is balanced, he lets go of her waist and lifts his arms to match hers. Make a clear picture together, then repeat the *enchaînement* on the other side.

Building up strength
You will not begin to study classical *pas de deux* until your final years of training, when you should be strong enough to dance the required steps. Before then, boys can do special exercises to build up their strength in the right way. These must be done only under strict supervision.

Lifting carefully
Zoltan has to concentrate hard throughout this lift. He has to make it look easy, and I help him as much as I can by pushing off well from a good *demi-plié*. To avoid damaging his back, he must hold it firmly when lifting, and keep his weight centred through his body.

Even during difficult lifts, the man must always think about the aesthetic look of his position and also the character he is portraying in the ballet.

Folk and character dancing

EVERY NATION has its own own collection of dances that are performed on formal and informal occasions. These dances, known as folk dances, may be taught in school, but many young people learn them from their elders, as part of growing up. They express all kinds of feelings and moods: from happy to sad, from exuberant to reflective. When danced in towns and villages, they may have rough edges, but they are full of spirit and commitment. Choreographers like to introduce folk dances into their ballets to add colour and movement, and to evoke the spirit of a particular nation or people. This stylized folk dancing is called character dancing.

Sabotière
This little French dance was specially choreographed for performing by the famous Russian ballet master Nicolai Legat. It tells the story of a girl and a boy meeting, dancing together, and finally stealing a kiss!

Coppélia
This is Sadler's Wells Royal Ballet (now The Birmingham Royal Ballet) performing *Coppélia*. In this ballet there are several character dances based on folk dances. They contain some of the steps of the original dances, but are modified and embellished to fit in with the style of the ballet. This is a dance from Act I based on a Polish mazurka.

Part of ballet
Character dancing will be part of your ballet training. You need to learn both disciplines and be able to move smoothly from one to the other. On stage, you may be dancing in this Russian style just before a beautiful *pas de deux* for a prince and princess.

These costumes for Sabotière are freely based on traditional designs from Brittany in France.

Many of the figures involve swinging your partner round.

Square dancing

This is one of the traditional dances found in the United States. It has developed from the country dances, round dances, square dances, and quadrilles of Europe. Traditionally, square dancing is led by a "caller" who chooses the figures and leads the dancers through them by singing, or "calling", instructions while the music is played.

The port de bras and footwork have considerable balletic qualities.

Scottish dancing

There are two forms of Scottish dancing: highland and country. Highland dancing is an ancient form, originally performed only by men. Some dances, such as the *Gillie Chalium*, begin slowly, but end more exuberantly. This matches the emotional feeling created by the music of the bagpipes. Country dancing is used in the ballroom, and is not classed as folk dancing.

Your dancing must be strong, but light and athletic.

Shoes for character-dancing classes are a lighter version of normal leather lace-up or strap shoes, but with special non-slip soles and heels.

The costumes are embroidered with traditional Celtic designs.

Irish dancing

The special quality of Irish dancing comes from the contrast between the controlled elegance of the body and the magical footwork. Although mostly based on simple movements, the steps can be elaborated in extraordinary ways. This is one of the intricate steps of a double jig, with syncopation and complex rhythms. The way you move across the floor and the rhythms you use are important and exciting.

In figure dancing and solos you may wear hard tapping shoes like these, or soft shoes for intricate footwork.

Mime and make-up

E VER SINCE Ancient Greek times, mime has been
used in the theatre as a way of expressing ideas,
feelings, and plots with gestures rather than words.
During its development, a number of gestures took on
particular meanings. Under the influence of early dancing
masters, some of these gestures became a part of ballet
choreography. This kind of mime is not used so much in
new ballets, but you will need to know a little about it to
understand and perform in the great ballets such as *Giselle*,
Swan Lake, and *The Sleeping Beauty*. It is
a small, but important part of
the ballet tradition, so
learn and enjoy it.

A serious art
Take your mimes seriously.
Do not exaggerate your
movements or be flippant.

Beg or beseech
Stand or kneel with your hands clasped
in front of you. Then bring your hands
close to you and bow your head.

Baby
You usually start a gesture with
your arms in a natural first or
second position. Slowly, with a
flowing movement, move your
arms into the specific gesture.
For this mime, bring your
arms together as if you were
gently cradling a baby.

Sleep for men
Put your hands
together against
your cheek and
rest your head
gently on them.

*Your gestures
should be beautiful
and harmonious, as
well as expressive.*

Mime with feeling
When performing the
gestures, draw your
audience into the story with
the power of your mime.

Sleep for women
Place your arms as if you were resting
on a table and close your eyes. When
miming, aim for simplicity, clarity,
and directness.

Kill

Pretend to take a dagger from its scabbard, raise it up into the air, and plunge it into your heart.

Make-up

Theatres today have powerful lights that are used creatively and dramatically. Make-up is therefore essential for dancers, to prevent them looking washed out or shiny. It is part of a dancer's art to make themselves up for different circumstances and characters.

3 Choose your lip colour according to the colour of the lights. For example, if the lights are very blue, red lipstick will look black. Pink would be better.

1 Choose a base colour for your face that is suitable for your character. Apply the make-up with a damp sponge. Blend it into your neck so that it does not look like a mask.

4 To make yourself up as a doll, like the famous one in Fokine's *Petrushka*, draw five or six "lashes" above your eyes with a black pencil.

2 Use eye make-up to make your eyes stand out from a distance. Ask a friend to tell you what it looks like. The effect is often quite different from a distance.

5 Then paint round red spots on your cheeks. Draw circles with a steady hand and fill them in.

6 Some false ringlets finish off the picture. Fix them firmly to your own hair with grips.

Wash make-up off
Water-based make-up allows you to wash it all off with soap and warm water. Always remove it straight after the show.

Although in mime you use your whole body expressively, the precise meaning is conveyed especially by your arms and hands.

Fright

This is the moment in *Swan Lake* (Act II) when, as the beautiful and tragic Princess Odette, I am startled by the sudden appearance of Prince Siegfried at the lakeside. Odette is frightened and wants to hide.

Preparing for a show

SCENERY and costumes have traditionally been an essential part of ballet. It is difficult to imagine *Les Sylphides* without the soft, dream-like white dresses and the mysterious woodland glade, or *Petrushka* without the fairground. So when you put on your own show, remember that the design of the ballet is as important as its music in creating its mood. From Leonardo da Vinci in the 16th century to Picasso in this century, great artists have been involved in ballet productions. Costumes have also developed – from the heavy bejewelled dresses of the early court days, to the tutus of the 19th century, to the body-tights of today. Designers are now able to draw on many styles to create productions for us to appreciate and enjoy.

A crown for a queen can be made from card painted gold.

A fairy's wings can be made of wire bent to shape and covered with gauze.

Costume

A ballet costume usually has to be worn for many performances, so it must be strong, comfortable, and safe. Take great care when you are trying on a costume. Make sure it fits properly and that it does not restrict your movements. It is useful if you can put it to the test in a dress-rehearsal.

Ask a friend to help you practise putting your headdress on. Get it just how you want it before the day of your performance.

Hair and headdress

Your hair, headdress, and make-up will make all the difference to how you look and also to how you dance. Choose something simple to suit the character you are playing. Make sure you can secure wigs or headdresses in your hair firmly. If you are confident that your appearance is right, you will be able to put all your thoughts and energy into your dancing.

The wardrobe mistress makes, alters, and cares for a school's costumes.

Improvise if you don't have something you need. These boots are laced with string.

Wardrobe

Many schools have a wardrobe department. It is an exciting place full of lycra, velvet, silk, chiffon, and perhaps even some suede, fake fur, or PVC. All this can be made up into costumes to fit the dancers. Extra dye colour, beads, braid, and ribbons can be used to change a costume dramatically for different productions.

Pieces of the material to be used are attached to the design.

This scenery is being painted for an English National Ballet production of Swan Lake.

Painting scenery

Some scenes have to be painted on huge pieces of cloth. The cloth is nailed to a frame and primed with white primer. The artists work from a small design divided into squares. They draw the design, square by square, on the cloth, which is divided into 1-metre squares. Next they mix colours from emulsion paint to match the colours of the design. Then they "lay in" the cloth using brushes from 7 to 15 centimetres wide. When the cloth is dry, the finishing touches are made from a small paint pallette.

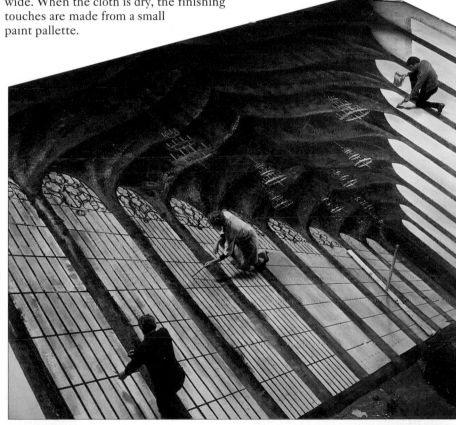

Costume design

These costume designs were for the Memphis Concert Ballet's (USA) 1993 production of the 19th-century ballet *Le Corsaire*. The notes down the side are from the artist and describe the costumes in detail. The designs are evocative and practical – two essential elements of good costume design.

Set design

The French painter and designer Christian Bérard did this set design for *Symphonie Fantastique* in 1936.

The Sleeping Princess

This design was by Bakst for the Diaghilev production of *The Sleeping Princess* in 1921. It shows an idea for the arrival of Prince Charming. Diaghilev was a major personality in the world of art and formed the Ballet Russe.

The show

ON THE DAY of the show, the choreographer will put the finishing touches to the new ballet after weeks of hard work. The expertise of many different people is needed to stage a ballet. Dancers, musicians, designers, stage staff, set builders, and dressmakers all have very responsible and specific roles to play. If you are in a show, make sure you are fully prepared. You do not want any last-minute panics on the first night.

On stage

Footlights

Downstage left	Downstage right
Upstage left	Upstage right

Wings ... **Wings**

Back cloth

Stage directions have names so that dancers can follow a choreographer's instructions. When you choreograph a ballet, find out the shape and size of the stage and arrange your dancers in a logical and balanced way. Rehearse on stage sometimes to get used to it. You can use tape to mark particular places.

A ballet to perform

Here is a ballet story to give you some ideas, or you can make up your own story.

The audience needs to see her despair.

Dance this with a dream-like quality.

Act I

Scene 1 A royal court
In a wonderful and magical land, there rules a king and queen. The prince, their son and heir, is betrothed to a lovely princess.

But the prince is in love with a poor serving maid and she with him. She realizes the hopelessness of her situation and decides to leave the castle.

The day for the marriage is arranged but the sad prince can think only of the serving maid. Her spirit is always with him.

Act II

Scene 1   A forest clearing
After many months of struggle and adventures, the prince and his friend stumble into a clearing in a forest. They see the serving maid sitting alone, wrapped in her own thoughts. The prince calls softly to her. She looks up at him and in that moment they realize that their lives are eternally bound together.

The first shy moment.

They dance a pas de deux, nervous and hesitant at first, becoming more passionate as it goes on. The prince persuades the maid to go back home to his kingdom with him.

Scene 2   The castle gardens
One day, guided by the Fairy of Happiness, the queen meets the maid in the castle garden. She immediately likes the girl and discovers the truth about the couple's love. She realizes she should allow them to marry.

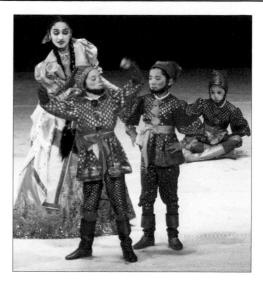

Joining the stars

You may be lucky enough to dance on stage with a professional ballet company. If you ever get this chance, you will enter a magic world full of colour and emotion, and the excitement will be unforgettable. These children are dancing with Georgette Farias of the Stuttgart Ballet in Germany in *The Sleeping Beauty*.

The final curtain

During the applause at the end of a performance, a ballerina often receives a gift of flowers. Then, as she makes her final graceful curtsies, the curtain falls and the performance is over.

Charmaine Hunter of the Dance Theatre of Harlem receives flowers and applause at the end of a performance of The Firebird.

This is a moment when you could use your knowledge of mime.

The fairy looks into the distance to "say" that it will be a hard and difficult journey.

Scene 2   A forest clearing

As the maid wanders in her sadness she meets the Fairy of Happiness and begs for help. The fairy promises to try to bring the couple together, but tells the maid that she must be patient.

Scene 3 The prince's rooms

The fairy appears to the prince in a dream. She tells him that he must go on a journey if he wants to find happiness.

The prince tells his friend about his dream. The friend advises him to follow the fairy's instructions and agrees to go with him on the journey. As they run off stage, the curtain falls on Act I.

Later the prince's friend, who has secretly loved the princess, is emboldened to declare his love. With a soft glance, the princess realizes she has found the man she always sought. They dance together, happy to have found each other.

Scene 3 The royal court

There is a double wedding. The two couples have the blessing of the king and queen and everyone enjoys the splendour and gaiety of the celebrations.

My life as a ballet dancer

BEING A PRINCIPAL ballerina is a wonderful experience and I enjoy all the challenges it presents. I dance in countries such as France, Russia, America, and Japan, as well as Britain and I am able to see the varied reactions the ballets receive from each culture. I love a dancer's life, but it is not easy. I have to work for perfection and remain in control for every performance. As a principal ballerina I dance with male principals from other countries and portray many differerent styles of *pas de deux*. I am fortunate to have performed in lots of the classic ballets, and to have learned other ballets, old and new, in The Royal Ballet's repertoire. Working on ballets with new choreographers and adapting to their individual styles is something I always look forward to.

Shoes are very personal because every dancer has different feet. I use both ribbons and elastic to keep my shoes secure.

Ballet shoes

As each ballet contains a number of different movements, I need more than one pair of ballet shoes. In scenes containing lots of jumping, I wear soft pointe shoes so that they do not make a noise when I land. For technical pointework, such as turning and balancing, I wear slightly harder shoes to give my feet more support. I try to rehearse steps in the same type of shoes I will use on stage.

I often prepare three or four pairs of ballet shoes for one performance.

Keeping my hair tidy

It is important for me to keep my hair up and out of the way, so that it does not distract me when I am rehearsing. Also, when I am rehearsing with a partner, I keep my hair tidy so that it does not go in his eyes.

Tutus

I only wear a tutu when performing classical ballets. I rehearse these ballets in a practice tutu so that my partner and I can get used to one.

Warming up

Warming up is essential before any rehearsal, because it is easy to strain cold muscles. To warm up I do lots of slow, repetitive stretching exercises for all the different muscle groups. Between rehearsals I wear legwarmers or a tracksuit to keep my muscles warm.

I wear a headdress to complement my costume. It has jewels that catch the light as I move. I have to make sure it is securely pinned to my hair before a performance.

Performing in Swan Lake

Swan Lake is one of the most challenging classical ballets in which I have performed. But at the same time it is very exhilarating. One minute I am the soft, white swan Odette, and the next I am the devious, black swan Odile. *Swan Lake* contains lots of difficult steps, and I need sustained confidence and stamina to perform them.

Rehearsing

I might have three or four rehearsals in a day for different ballets. When rehearsing my solos, I have to repeat some steps again and again until they are perfect. My teacher guides me to improve some of the harder movements. Some steps can require several weeks of practice before I am happy with them.

The detail on my tutu is light and subtle, but sufficient to portray the character I am playing. The white feathers represent the white swan Odette.

Hard work

My partner and I must trust each other because a lot of the *pas de deux* moves in *Swan Lake*, and other ballets, are difficult. They can be dangerous if performed half-heartedly. We therefore have to prepare the *pas de deux* movements very carefully.

Other dance forms

BALLET IS only one of many dance forms. Some are first and foremost social activities that anyone can enjoy, regardless of physique or age. But if you want to dance seriously you will need to have lessons. There are classes in most kinds of dancing. Contemporary dancing is a freer form of artistic dancing than ballet, and plays a big part in the way dancing is taught in most schools today. There are also the forms of dancing connected to jazz, the theatre, and popular music. As you explore any of these, or other forms of dancing, you will discover that each has its own experts and traditions, and is a study of its own.

Tap shoes have toe and heel taps fitted. These make the special sound on the floor.

Jazz dancing

This style of dancing is a North American tradition that developed from a mixture of African and European dances. Today it is used extensively in musicals, and is often referred to as show, or commercial, dancing.

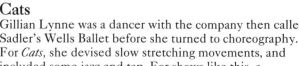

Jazz dancing is lively and fun and full of colour and rhythm.

Contemporary dancing

What we call contemporary dancing is now nearly 100 years old. It started with the American "modern" dancers Isadora Duncan and Loïe Fuller. They devised what they felt was a freer and more natural form of expressive dancing. Martha Graham and Merce Cunningham, among others, later developed specific traditions of contemporary dancing, each with its own technique, style, and training.

Cats

Gillian Lynne was a dancer with the company then called Sadler's Wells Ballet before she turned to choreography. For *Cats,* she devised slow stretching movements, and included some jazz and tap. For shows like this, a classical ballet training is invaluable.

Use the whole of your body to tap dance, not just your feet and ankles.

Tap dancing

Like jazz, tap is an American art that has its roots in slavery. The African slaves mixed their traditional dances with the jigs and clog dances of the white people. So was born a new tapping, swinging style of dancing, which is performed throughout the world.

You will need to move quickly and rhythmically to tap dance. For this, it is important that you understand where your centre of balance is.

Starlight Express

Modern musicals can make all kinds of demands on dancers. *Starlight Express*, choreographed by Arlene Phillips, is famous for the dancers' daredevil acrobatics and circus stunts – all on roller skates!

42nd Street

The overture ends and the curtain rises just enough for the audience to see 30 pairs of tapping feet! The choreographer of *42nd Street*, Gower Champion, used bold theatrical effects like this to pay homage to the dancers of the 1930s such as Fred Astaire.

Gesture in contemporary dancing is, in its own way, as evocative as gesture in ballet.

In contemporary dancing, you can be inventive with the use of movements on the floor.

The movements in contemporary dancing are expressive and supple.

Contemporary dancers often dance barefoot.

Choreography

A CHOREOGRAPHER'S role in ballet is like that of a composer's in music, or an artist's in painting. But unlike a composer or a painter, the choreographer's materials are living people. The choreographer decides on the theme of the ballet, its music, and its story, and creates steps for the dancers to perform. Often a ballet is created for specific dancers, with steps that show off the dancers' particular talents. Great choreographers, such as Petipa, Balanchine, and Ashton all developed their own distinctive styles, and the companies of dancers with whom they worked became especially expert and experienced in performing their works.

Bintley
After deciding on the theme, the music, and the story for a ballet, a choreographer will imagine the movements and try them out with dancers. Here, David Bintley is showing dancers what he wants for his ballet *The Swan of Tuonela*. Bintley is one of today's most exciting choreographers. His work is sensitive and wide-ranging, covering many styles and themes.

"Still Life" at the Penguin Café
One of David Bintley's ballets is *"Still Life" at the Penguin Café*. He set it to fascinating and unusual music by Simon Jeffes. It is a thought-provoking ballet, both touching and funny. Through dance, Bintley makes the audience think about the consequences of allowing animals to become extinct.

Bintley's choreography conjures up a zebra, performed by Phillip Broomhead, wandering in the whispering grasses of the African savannah.

The monkey's very essence is captured by the movements created for Stephen Jefferies.

Benesh notation

Until this century, there was no secure way of recording the steps of ballet. Ballets were passed on by dancers and choreographers through memory. Because of this, many early ballets have been lost. During this century, a number of different ways of notating dance have been developed. This is called choreology. One of the most popular is Benesh notation. It is named after Rudolf and Joan Benesh, who invented it in the late 1940s. Benesh notation is written on a five-line stave, like a music stave. It is placed below the music stave so that both the music and the movement can be read together.

Benesh notation for arabesque

Head turned to right and slightly tilted back

Right hand in front at head height

Top of head

Shoulder line

Left hand behind, just above waist height

Waist line

Knee line

Right foot behind at hip height

Floor line

Left knee bent and turned out

Dancer is standing on flat of left foot.

Dancer is facing stage left.

The arabesque indicated by the Benesh notation

Balanchine

George Balanchine (1904-1983) created more than 100 ballets, including *Serenade*, *Apollo*, *The Four Temperaments*, and *Symphony in C*. Born and trained in Russia, he moved to New York, USA, in 1933, after working in Europe. He devised a new classic style, part Russian and part American. His ballets are often abstract in theme or without a plot. They are both athletic and graceful, complex and clear. Balanchine is shown here working closely with his dancers.

Members of the Kirov Ballet in Apollo. *Apollo and his muses form a clean but complex pattern as they urge him towards beauty.*

Keeping ballet alive

Ballets choreographed many years ago are still performed today by different companies all over the world. Obviously, the choreographer of a ballet cannot always be there to show the dancers what to do. Although ballets can now be recorded on film or by notation, full knowledge of how to perform them can only be handed on from one dancer to another. The tradition of teaching is therefore a vital link between the past and the future.

Patricia Neary rehearsing Apollo *with the Kirov Ballet*

Apollo

In 1928, *Apollo* marked the arrival of Balanchine as a great choreographer. He brought back into ballet a purity of line and gesture that had long been lost. This is one of the 12 ballets that Balanchine choreographed to Stravinsky's music. Balanchine maintained that his Apollo was not the traditional perfect god, but "a wild half-human youth who acquires nobility through art".

Les Sylphides

It now seems that this is the classic Romantic *ballet blanc*, or white ballet, steeped in feminine beauty and lovely, gauzy costumes. Yet it was not created in the 1840s, as were most of the Romantic ballets, but in 1908, by Michel Fokine in Russia. It was originally called *Chopiniana*, and still is in Russia, because it is danced to music by Chopin. Although it has no plot, the dancers suggest a moonlit romance. This eight-bar phrase in Benesh notation is from the prelude solo of Fokine's ballet, leading up to the quiet moment shown in the picture.

Natalia Makarova as a guest dancer with The Royal Ballet in Les Sylphides.

Going to the ballet

ONE OF THE EXCITING things about watching ballet is the variety of different styles. You can enter the mysterious world of heroes and sylphs in the Romantic ballets, or see the grandeur and jewel-like splendour of Petipa's work. Then there are the exotic ballets of the Diaghilev era, with brilliant dancers, musicians, and designers, or the clear beauty of Balanchine. You can absorb the culture, poetry, and humour of Ashton, or the drama and psychological power of MacMillan. Or you may prefer modern ballets, which experiment with forms and feelings. When you buy your ticket for the ballet, make sure that you will be able to see the stage clearly. If you have a seat high up in the theatre, you will be able to see all the floor patterns the dancers are making, as well as their entrances and exits. Here are some ballets you can look out for.

The Australian Ballet

Suite en blanc
This ballet without a story was choreographed by Lifar to music by Lalo and was first performed in Paris in 1943. It involves a large company. The girls wear white tutus and the men wear white shirts. The stage is divided into two tiers and the possibilities of movement are fully exploited.

Les Noces (The Wedding)
This ballet is a remarkable piece of dance theatre. It was first performed in 1923 and was very unlike a conventional ballet. Originally choreographed by Bronislava Nijinska, with music and song lyrics by Stravinsky, *Les Noces* represents a Russian peasant wedding with great vigour, power, and earthiness. The version shown here was choreographed by Jiri Kylian.

The Bavarian Ballet

The Frankfurt Ballet

Steptext
This ballet is only 17 minutes long. It was choreographed by William Forsythe, one of the most exciting choreographers in the world today. Deriving from classical ballet, his works push both the language of dance and the dancers themselves to new extremes.

Petrushka
Representing a crowded fairground, Fokine's *Petrushka* captures all the movement and excitement of the fair. In one booth, a magician makes three dolls dance. At dusk, in the back of their booth, the dolls come alive.

The Royal Ballet

Touchbase
This a modern ballet choreographed by Merce Cunningham on dancers from the Rambert Dance Company. Cunningham is a leading figure in experimental dance. His work aims to show human movement in all its variety.

Rambert Dance Company

Romeo and Juliet

Many choreographers, including Sir Frederick Ashton and Sir Kenneth MacMillan, have choreographed versions of this ballet based on Shakespeare's play. The music most often used today is that of Sergei Prokoviev.

The Dance Theatre of Harlem

Margot Fonteyn and Rudolf Nureyev were the first stars of MacMillan's ballet made for The Royal Ballet.

The programme
Try to read the programme before the performance begins. Even if the ballet does not have a story, there will be lots of information about the music, the dancers, and the choreographers. The more you know about what you are watching, the more you will enjoy it.

The Four Temperaments

This ballet by Balanchine has no plot. It is based on the medieval idea that a human being contains four humours: the melancholic (gloomy), the sanguine (cheerful), the phlegmatic (inexcitable), and the choleric (angry). Between the ballet's opening theme and finale, each humour has its own variation.

The Sleeping Beauty

This is the classic full-length fairy-tale ballet, with court scenes, good and bad fairies, a beautiful princess, and a brave, handsome prince. It was originally choreographed by Marius Petipa in 1890, but there have been many versions since. *The Sleeping Beauty* is the supreme classical ballet. It represents the ultimate challenge for a classical ballerina.

The Royal Ballet

Moscow Classical Ballet

A Month in the Country

Sir Frederick Ashton choreographed this ballet in 1976. It is based on a play by Ivan Turgenev. Ashton compressed humour, passion, drama, character, and the atmosphere of a lazy summer holiday all into one act.

Useful addresses

Studying dancing can be very enjoyable, whether you want to dance as a hobby or as a career. If you want to go to a professional school, you will have to audition because a particular type of body and motivation are needed for a professional training. Below are the addresses of some schools and companies.

The Arts Educational London School
Cone Ripman House
14 Bath Road
Chiswick
London W4 1LY
0181 994 9366

The Benesh Institute of Choreology
12 Lisson Grove
London NW1 6TS
071 258 3041

The Birmingham Royal Ballet
Birmingham Hippodrome
Thorp Street
Birmingham B5 4AU
0121 622 2555

Central School of Ballet
10 Herbal Hill
Clerkenwell Road
London EC1 5EJ
0171 837 6332

Doreen Bird College of Theatre Dance
Birkbeck Centre
Birkbeck Road
Sidcup
Kent DA14 4DE
0181 300 6004

Stephen Jefferies in "Still Life" *at the* Penguin Café *for The Royal Ballet.*

A ballet class at the Royal Ballet School

Elmhurst Ballet School
Heathcote Road
Camberley
Surrey GU15 2HS
0276 65301

English National Ballet School
Markova House
39 Jay Mews
London SW7 2ES
0171 581 1245

Hammond School
Reliance House
3rd Floor
Waterloo Road
Chester CH2 2AL
0244 383849

Laban Centre for Movement and Dance
Laurie Grove
New Cross
London
SE14 6NH
0181 692 4070

London City Ballet
42-50 York Way
London N1 9AB
0171 837 3133

London Contemporary Dance School
The Place
17 Duke's Road
London WC1H 9AB
0171 387 0152

London Studio Centre
42-50 York Way
London N1 9AB
0171 837 7741

Northern Ballet School
The Dance House
10a Oxford Road
Manchester M1 5QA
0161 237 1406

Rambert Dance Company
94 Chiswick High Road
London W4 1SH
0181 995 4246

Rambert School
West London Institute of Higher Education
Gordon House
300 St Margaret's Road
Twickenham
Middlesex TW1 1PT
0181 891 0121

Royal Academy of Dancing (College of)
36 Battersea Square
London SW11 3RA
0171 223 0091

The Royal Ballet
Royal Opera House
Covent Garden
London WC2E 9DD
0171 240 1200

Royal Ballet School (Lower)
White Lodge
Richmond Park
Surrey TW10 5HR
0181 878 3929

Royal Ballet School (Upper)
155 Talgarth Road
London W14 9DE
0181 748 6335

The Scottish Ballet Ltd
261 West Princes Street
Glasgow G4 9EE
0141 331 2931

Further information
If you would like a more comprehensive list of dance schools throughout the UK, write to the following address enclosing a stamped addressed envelope:

Council for Dance Education and Training (UK)
Riverside Studios
Crisp Road
London W6 9RL
081 741 5084

Details of a selection of ballets

Apollo (1928)
Music: Stravinsky
Choreography: Balanchine
Follows Apollo from his birth, through his education, to his final ascent of Mount Parnassus.

L'Après-midi d'un faune (1912)
Music: Debussy
Choreography: Nijinsky
A faun, playing on his flute one summer afternoon, falls in love with a nymph.

La Bayadère (1877)
Music: Minkus
Choreography: Petipa
Tells of a love triangle between the bayadère Nikya, Solor, and Gamzatti.

Fiona Chadwick and Jonathan Cope in La Bayadère.

Cinderella
Music: Prokofiev
Choreography: versions by Ashton and others
Based on Perrault's famous fairy tale about the love of Cinderella and Prince Charming despite interference from the two ugly sisters.

Coppélia (1870)
Music: Delibes
Choreography: Saint-Léon
Combines the story of the romance between Swanilda and Franz with the story of the doll-maker Coppelius, who tries to create a doll with a soul, called Coppélia.

Le Corsaire (1856)
Music: Adam and others
Choreography: Mazilier
Based on Lord Byron's poem *The Corsair* about a Greek girl sold into slavery.

The Dream (1964)
Music: Mendelssohn
Choreography: Ashton
Roughly following the plot of Shakespeare's *A Midsummer Night's Dream*, it centres around an argument between Titania and Oberon over a mysterious Indian boy and the loves of Helena.

Elite Syncopations (1974)
Music: S Joplin and others
Choreography: MacMillan
Ragtime ballet set in a dance hall.

The Firebird (1910)
Music: Stravinsky
Choreography: Fokine
Based on various Russian fairy tales, it tells of Prince Ivan who captures the Firebird.

Giselle (1841)
Music: Adam
Choreography: Coralli and Perrot
Follows the romance between Giselle, a peasant girl, and Albrecht, a count.

Medea (1950)
Music: Bartók
Choreography: Cullberg
Ballet of love and revenge, based on an Ancient Greek legend.

A Month in the Country (1976)
Music: Chopin
Choreography: Ashton
Based on a play by Turgenev about the love-triangle between Natalia Petrovna, her ward Vera, and a tutor, Beliaev.

Les Noces (1923)
Music: Stravinsky
Choreography: Nijinska
Based on a Russian wedding ritual.

The Nutcracker (1892)
Music: Tchaikovsky
Choreography: Ivanov
Klara is given a nutcracker for Christmas. At night, all her gifts come to life.

Petrushka (1911)
Music: Stravinsky
Choreography: Fokine
The owner of a puppet theatre has three puppets, Petrushka, the Ballerina, and the Moor, who come to life.

The Prince of the Pagodas (1957)
Music: Britten
Choreography: Cranko
Fairy-tale ballet about the Emperor of the Middle Kingdom and his two daughters.

Romeo and Juliet
Music: Prokofiev
Choreography: versions by Ashton, MacMillan, and others
Follows Shakespeare's tragedy of social conflict.

The Sleeping Beauty (1890)
Music: Tchaikovsky
Choreography: Petipa
Based on Perrault's famous fairy tale.

Solitaire (1956)
Music: Arnold
Choreography: MacMillan
Concerns a girl who repeatedly tries to join in the activities of her friends, but always finds herself left alone.

Steptext (1984)
Music: Bach
Choreography: Forsythe
Ballet which pushes both the art form and the dancers to new extremes.

"Still Life" at the Penguin Café (1988)
Music: Jeffes
Choreography: Bintley
Ballet which makes us think about the environment.

Swan Lake (1895)
Music: Tchaikovsky
Choreography: Petipa/Ivanov
Tells the story of Princess Odette, who is turned into a swan.

Les Sylphides (1907)
Music: Chopin
Choreography: Fokine
A young man dances with the spirits of young women.

Tales of Beatrix Potter (1971)
Music: Lanchbery
Choreography: Ashton
Ballet in which the best loved of Beatrix Potter's characters are portrayed.

Theme and Variations (1947)
Music: Tchaikovsky
Choreography: Balanchine
Plotless ballet set to the final movement of Tchaikovsky's *Suite No. 3* in G major.

Touchbase (1992)
Music: Pugioese
Choreography: Cunningham
Ballet that looks at human movement in all its variety.

Glossary

You will find many of the words on these pages useful during your ballet classes.

A

Adage Derived from the musical term *adagio*, meaning at ease or leisure. Slow and graceful movements.

Air, en l' In the air. When the working leg is in the air.

Allegro Taken from the Italian musical term meaning brisk and lively. Lively movements.

Allongé Extended or outstretched.

Arabesque A pose on one leg with the other leg extended behind and the body forming a graceful curve.

Arrière, en Backwards. When a step is performed backwards, away from the audience.

Assemblé Assembled. A jump in which the legs are brought together in the air before landing in fifth position.

Attitude A pose on one leg with the other leg lifted either backwards or forwards and bent at the knee.

Avant, en Forwards. When a step is performed forwards, towards the audience.

B

Ballet blanc White ballet. Any ballet in which the dancers wear traditional long white dresses, as designed for Marie Taglioni to wear in *La Sylphide* in 1830.

Ballet d'action A ballet with a story.

Ballon Bounce. The right elastic quality of a jump.

Ballonné A bouncing jump in which the dancer lands on one leg in *demi-plié* with the working foot *sur le cou de pied*.

Barre The hand rail used by dancers to help them balance while exercising.

Barrework Initial exercises of daily classroom work, performed at the barre.

Battement Beating. A beating action of the working leg when extended or bent. There are many types of battement, small and large.

Battement frappé A strong striking movement of the working leg away from *cou de pied* to a low extended position in front, to the side, or behind.

Battement tendu A movement in which the working leg is stretched along the floor to a fully extended position.

Battement tendu jeté A movement in which the working leg is "thrown" into the air at a low height.

Batterie Beating. Movements in which the legs beat against each other in the air. There are many different types.

Bras Arm.

C

Centre of balance An imaginary line through your body on which you are evenly balanced in a particular pose.

Centre practice Exercises performed in the centre of the room away from the barre.

Character dancing A style of dancing derived from national, traditional, or folk dances.

Changement de pieds Changing feet. A small or large jump in which the feet change position in the air.

Choreographer The person who composes or invents a ballet or dance, and arranges the steps.

Choreography The actual steps and patterns of a ballet or dance.

Choreology The recording of ballet in notation form.

Classical ballet The traditional ballet technique. Also: A ballet from the second half of the 19th century that displays the classical technique.

Contemporary dancing A modern style of dancing that is freer than classical ballet.

Corps de ballet A group of dancers who perform, usually as a group, in support of the soloists and leading dancers.

Cou de pied Neck of the foot. A position of the working foot on or around the ankle of the supporting leg.

Croisé Crossed. A position in which the body is turned slightly and the line of the legs is crossed to the audience.

D

Dedans, en Inwards. When a movement, step, or turn of the body is towards the supporting leg.

Dégagé Disengaged. When the foot is pointed in an open position with a fully arched instep.

Dehors, en Outwards. When a movement, step, or turn of the body is away from the supporting leg.

Demi-plié Half-bend. A position in which the knees are half bent.

Demi-pointes Half-points. When a dancer stands on the ball of their feet.

Derrière Behind. When a movement, step, or placing of an arm or leg is done behind the body.

Dessous Under. When the working foot passes behind the supporting foot.

Dessus Over. When the working foot passes in front of the supporting foot.

Devant In front. When a movement, step, or placing of an arm or leg is done in front of the body.

Développé Developed. An unfolding movement of the working leg into an open position in the air.

Divertissement Diversion, enjoyment. Short dances inserted into a classic ballet to display the talents of individuals or groups of dancers.

E

Ecarté Separated or thrown wide apart. A basic pose in which a dancer's leg is in second position, but the whole body is placed diagonally to the audience.

Echappée Escaped. A movement of both legs simultaneously into an open position, performed on the floor or in the air.

Effacé A position in which the body is turned slightly, and the line of the legs is open to the audience.

Elévation Height. The height achieved in any jumping movement.

Enchaînement Linking. A number of steps linked together.

Epaulement   Shouldered. A particular and artistic placing of the shoulders, head, and body as a dancer turns a little towards or away from the audience.

F

Face, en   Facing. When a dancer faces straight out to the audience.
Fermé   Closed. When the feet are in a closed position.
Folk dancing   A type of dancing that has developed through the traditions of a culture, and been passed down from generation to generation.
Fondu   Melting. A smooth melting movement.
Frappé   Struck. As, for example, in *battement frappé.*

G

Grand   Large. As, for example, in *grand allegro.*

Grand allegro   The larger jumps and travelling steps of *allegro.*
Grand battement   A quick and energetic "throw" of the leg into the air.
Grande échappée   A version of the jump *échappée sautée*, in which the legs are opened only at the moment of the return to the floor.
Grand jeté   A big jump from one leg to the other, with legs outstretched in the air.
Grand plié   A position in which the legs are fully bent.

J

Jambe   Leg.
Jazz dancing   A style of dancing that developed in North America, from a mixture of African and European folk dances.
Jeté   Thrown. As, for example, in *battement jeté.*

M

Modern ballet   A type of ballet from this century.

N

Notation   Various systems of recording the choreography of ballets in writing, including Benesh notation and Labanotation.
Nuance   A slight or subtle difference, which alters the meaning or effect.

O

Ouvert   Open. When the feet are in an open position to the audience.

P

Parterre   On the ground. As, for example, in *rond de jambe parterre.*
Pas   Step. As, for example, in *pas de chat.*
Pas de bourrée   Step of the Bourrée. An old French dance refined and developed in classical ballet. It takes many forms but involves changing from one foot to the other several times.
Pas de chat   Step of a cat. A jump in various forms that resembles the steps of a cat.
Pas couru   Running step. A travelling step composed of small running steps of varied forms.
Pas de deux   A dance for two people.
Pas glissade   A gliding step that can be either jumped or taken smoothly up to pointe.
Penché   Leaning or tilted. As, for example, in *arabesque penchée* when the raised leg goes very high as the body leans fowards.
Petit   Small. As, for example, in *petit battement.*
Petit allegro   The smaller jumps and travelling steps of *allegro.*
Petit battement   Fast, small beats of the working leg in front of and behind the supporting leg.
Petite échappée   A version of the jump *échappée sautée*, in which the legs are opened in the air before returning to the floor.
Pied   Foot.
Pirouette   Spinning top. A particular way of turning on one leg.
Placing   The way the body is held according to the rules of classical ballet.
Plié   Bent. A bending of the knee or knees.
Port de bras   Carriage of the arms. A movement of the arms to and through various positions.
Pointe tendue   Point stretched. When the leg is extended and stretched so that only the tip of the toes are on the floor.
Pointes, sur les   On the points. The raising of the body on to the tip of the toes.
Pose   A pose or particular position of classical ballet.
Préparation   Preparation. The movement with which a dancer prepares to dance.
Principal   A leading dancer in a ballet company.

R

Relevé   Raised. A movement in which the body is raised up on to pointes or *demi-pointes.*

Retiré   Withdrawn. When the toes of the working leg are raised from a closed position to a point just below the knee.
Révérence   Curtsey. A curtsey or bow performed at the end of a class or performance.
Romantic ballet   A style of ballet from the Romantic period in the first half of the 19th century.
Rond de jambe   Circle of the leg. A circular movement of the leg.
Rosin   A powder made from the sap of fir trees, which dancers put on the soles of their shoes to stop them from slipping.

S

Sauté   Jumped. When a movement is performed with a jump as, for example, in *échappée sautée.*
Seconde, à la   To the second. When the leg is in second position on the floor or in the air.
Simple   Ordinary. As, for example, in *sissonne simple.*
Sissonne   A special sort of jump from two feet that can be danced in many ways.
Sissonne simple   A jump from two feet landing in *cou de pied devant* or *derrière.*
Soloist   A dancer who performs on their own.
Soutenu   Sustained.
Spotting   The movement of the head in pirouettes and other particular ways of turning.
Sur   On or upon. As, for example, in *sur les pointes.*
Sur place   On the spot.
Syncopation   The stressing of the parts of the rhythm of a piece of music in between the strong beats.

T

Tap dancing   A style of dancing developed in North America, involving quick tapping of the toes and heels on the floor.
Temps levé   Time raised. A hop on one foot.
Temps lié   Time bound together. A sequence of movements connected together smoothly.
Tendu   Stretched. As, for example, in *battement tendu.*
Tour en l'air   Turn in the air.
Tournant, en   Turning. When a step is done moving round.
Turnout   The way the feet and legs should be turned out from the hip joints to give the necessary freedom of movement to perform the steps of classical ballet.

Index

A
adage 20, 21, 27, 62
  supported 42
Adam, Adolphe 61
allegro 34, 36, 37, 62, 63
Apollo 57, 61
Après-midi d'un faune, l' 61
arabesques 21, 22, 28-29, 42, 56, 62, 63
arms
  basic positions 13, 27
Arnold, Malcolm 61
Ashton, Frederick 36, 56, 58, 59, 61
assemblé 62
Astaire, Fred 55
attitudes 21, 27, 36, 41, 62
Australian Ballet, The 58

B
Bach, Johann 61
Bakst, Léon 49
balance, 16, 18, 20, 21, 23, 28, 33, 37, 39, 40, 42, 52
  centre of 11, 15, 28, 32, 33, 42, 55, 62
Balanchine, George 25, 56, 57, 58, 59, 61
ballet blanc 57, 62
ballet d'action 62
Ballet Russe 49
ballon 37, 62
ballonné 36-37
barre 10, 11, 62
  how to hold 14, 18
barrework 12, 14-15, 16-17, 18-19, 20-21, 23, 31, 39, 62
Bartók, Béla 61
battements 16-17, 18-19, 62, 63
  fondu 18-19, 20
  frappé 20, 62
  grand battement 21, 62, 63
  petit battement 20, 63
  tendu 16-17, 27, 30, 62
Bavarian Ballet, The 58
Bayadère, La 37, 61
bending 22-23, 24, 25, 31
Benesh notation 56-57
Benesh, Rudolf and Joan 56
Berard, Christian 49
Bintley, David 56, 61
Birmingham Royal Ballet, The 29, 36, 44
Britten, Benjamin 61
Broomhead, Phillip 56

C
Cats 54
centre practice 11, 12, 15, 16, 26-27, 28-29, 30-31, 32-33, 39, 62
Chadwick, Fiona 37
Champion, Gower 55
character dancing 6, 44-45, 62
Chopin, Frédérik 61
choreographers 44, 52, 54, 55, 59, 61, 62
choreography 7, 25, 46, 50, 54, 55, 56-57, 62
choreology 56, 62
Cinderella 61

classes 8, 10, 11, 12, 14, 16, 23, 34, 40, 44, 54
classical ballets 62
clothes 8-9
contemporary dancing 54-55, 62
Cope, Jonathan 37
Coppélia 44, 61
Coralli, Jean 61
corps de ballet 62
Corsaire, Le 49, 61
costumes 8, 45, 48
  making your own 48
cou de pied 18, 19, 20, 31, 32, 35, 37, 62
Cranko, John 61
Cullberg, Birgit 61
Cunningham, Merce 54, 58, 61

D
da Vinci, Leonardo 48
dance companies 60
Dance Theatre of Harlem 22, 51, 59
Debussy, Claude 61
Delibes, Clément 61
développé 20, 21, 62
Diaghilev, Sergei 49, 58
Dream, The 61
Duncan, Isadora 54

E
elévation 62
Elite Syncopations 40, 41, 61
enchaînements 42-43, 63
English National Ballet 49

F
Farias, Georgette 51
feet
  basic positions 13, 34
Fille mal Gardée, La 36
Firebird, The 51, 61
Fokine, Michel 47, 57, 58, 61
folk dancing 6, 44-45, 63
Fonteyn, Margot 59
Forsythe, William 58, 61
42nd Street 55
Four Temperaments, The 57, 59
Frankfurt Ballet, The 58
Fuller, Loïe 54

G
Giselle 46, 61
Graham, Martha 54
grand jeté 36, 37, 63
Grisi, Carlotta 7

H
hair 8, 47, 48, 52, 53
hands
  basic position 24
  allongées 24, 31, 32, 62
history of ballet 7, 10, 38, 42, 46, 48
Houston Ballet 25
Hunter, Charmaine 51

I
Irish dancing 45
Ivanov, Lev 61

J
Jacobsson, Petter 29
jazz dancing 54, 63
Jefferies, Stephen 56

Jeffes, Simon 56, 61
Joplin, Scott 40, 61
jumping 6, 18, 27, 30, 34-35, 36-37, 52
  preparing for 34, 35

K
Kirov Ballet 57
Kylian, Jiri 58

L
Lalo, Edouard-Victor-Antoine 58
Lanchbery, John 61
Legat, Nicolai 44
Lifar, Serge 58
lifting 27, 42, 43
Louis XIV, King 10
Lynne, Gillian 54

M
MacMillan, Kenneth 40, 41, 58, 59, 61
Makarova, Natalia 57
make-up 46
masques 7
Mazilier, Joseph 61
Medea 22, 61
Memphis Concert Ballet 49
Mendelssohn, Felix 61
miming 46-47, 51
Minkus, Alois 61
modern ballets 63
Month in the Country, A 59, 61
Moscow Classical Ballet 59
music 10, 11, 18, 19, 24, 25, 31, 45, 54, 56, 57, 58, 59, 61

N
Neary, Patricia 57
Nijinska, Bronislava 58, 61
Nijinsky, Vaslav 61
Noces, Les 58, 61
notation 56-57, 63
Nureyev, Rudolf 59
Nutcracker, The 26, 61

P
pas ballonné 41
pas couru 30-31, 63
pas de bourrée 31, 63
pas de chat 37, 63
pas de deux 7, 42-43, 44, 50, 52, 53, 63
pas dégagé 30
pas échappé 39
pas échappée sautée 35
pas glissade 39, 63
Perrot, Jules 61
Petipa, Marius 56, 58, 59, 61
Petrushka 47, 48, 58, 61
Phillips, Arlene 55
Picasso, Pablo 48
pirouettes 32-33, 63
pliés 14-15, 63
  demi- 14, 15, 17, 19, 30, 31, 32, 33, 34, 35, 36, 37, 39, 41, 43, 62
  grand 14, 15, 63
pointe tendue 42, 63
pointework 6, 18, 38-39, 40-41, 42
port de bras 24-25, 41, 45, 63
poses 26-27, 32, 63
preparatory position 12, 15, 18, 20, 24, 25, 31, 32
Prince of the Pagodas, The 61
Prokofiev, Serge 59, 61

Pugilese, Michael 61

R
Rambert Dance Company 58
rehearsing 23, 43, 48, 50, 52, 53
relevés 14-15, 20, 21, 33, 38, 39, 40, 41, 63
retiré position 20, 32, 33, 63
révérences 11, 63
Romantic ballets 38, 57, 58, 63
Romantic period 7
Romeo and Juliet 59, 61
ronds de jambe 17, 20, 63
rosin 38, 63
Royal Ballet, The 26, 52, 57, 58, 59

S
Sabotière 44-45
Sadler's Wells Royal Ballet 44, 54
Saint-Léon, Arthur 61
scenery 48, 49
schools 60
Scottish dancing 45
Serenade 25, 57
shoes 6, 9, 38, 52
  character 45
  flat 8
  pointe 8, 9, 39, 40, 52
  tap 54
  darning pointes 9
  sewing on elastic/ribbons 8, 39
  tying ribbons 9, 38
sissonnes 35, 36, 63
  fondue 36
  simple 35, 63
Sleeping Beauty, The 46, 51, 59, 61
Sleeping Princess, The 49
Solitaire 61
Solymosi, Zoltan 40, 43
spotting 32, 63
square dancing 45
stage directions 50
Starlight Express 55
Steptext 58, 61
"*Still Life" at the Penguin Café* 56, 61
Stravinsky, Igor 57, 58, 61
stretching 22
studios 10
Stuttgart Ballet 51
Suite en blanc 58
Swan Lake 7, 43, 46, 47, 49, 53, 61
Swan of Tuonela 56
Sylphides, Les 48, 57, 61
Symphonie Fantastique 49
Symphony in C 57

T
Tales of Beatrix Potter 35, 61
tap dancing 55, 63
Tchaikovsky, Piotr 61
teachers 8, 9, 10, 11, 20, 23, 24, 29, 35, 53, 57
temps levé 34, 63
temps lié 31, 63
Theme and Variations 29, 61
Touchbase 58, 61
Trevitt, William 35
turning 27, 31, 32-33, 52
tutus 9, 48, 52, 53, 58

W
warming up 10, 23, 52

Y
Yoshida, Miyako 29, 36

Lara   Lisa   Robert   Anna   Darcey   Oliver   Nandita   Georgina   Alex   Elizabeth

Acknowledgments

Dorling Kindersley would like to thank the following people
for their help in the production of this book:

All the Young Dancers for giving up their spare time to be photographed for this book; Victoria Hewitt, Martin Howland, and Bennet Gartside for performing other dance forms for photography; Danielle Greenhalgh for providing an idea for a ballet story; all the staff at White Lodge, especially Carole Leicester for her help with the wardrobe; Amanda Jones at The Royal Ballet for her help and cooperation; Adrian Grater for his help with the Benesh notation; Dancia International of Drury Lane for lending clothes; Claire Bampton for editorial assistance; Susan St Louis for design assistance; Kathy Lockley for Picture Research.

Darcey Bussell would like to thank:
Anthony Dowell for all his guidance in my career; my parents for always being there when I need help; and all the people who have trained and encouraged me so far.

Patricia Linton would like to thank:
Anatole Grigoriev for his support, and help with placing the dancers for photography; Dame Merle Park, Rashna Homji-Jefferies, Shirley Grahame,

Christine Beckley, and Janet Briggs for their comments on parts of the text; also, for their advice and comments: Carole Leicester on costumes, Ron Smedley and Bob Parker on American square dancing, William Ireland on Scottish dancing, Joy Ransley on Irish dancing, Bill Drysdale on tap and jazz, Ross McKim on contemporary dancing, Fred le Conte on set painting, and Guy Attew on musicals; Audrey Harman, the Royal Ballet School archivist; and finally Nicole Vlasto for checking the French.

Picture credits
key: B bottom; L left; R right; C centre; T top.
Bridgeman Art Library: 49BL
Camera Press/Anthony Crickmay: 7BR, 40BL, 40R, 43, 53BR, 53L
Dee Conway: 55CL
English National Ballet: 49CR, 49TR
Nan Melville: 49TL. 49CL, 51TR, 57C, 58CR, 58CL; /Choreography by George Balanchine. © The George Balanchine Trust: 25C, 57TR
Rex Features: 54BL, 55CR
Linda Rich: 29TR, 35TR, 37T, 58BR, 60CL

Leslie E Spatt: 36C, 51TL, 56CL, 58CR, 59BL, 60BL; /Choreography by George Balanchine. Used by permission of Copyright Owner, Edward Bigelow: 50CL
Martha Swope Associates/Carol Rosegg: 22CL
Reg Wilson: 26TR, 29TR, 44C, 56TR, 57BR, 58C, 58TR, 59TC; /Choreography by George Balanchine. © The George Balanchine Trust: 57TL.

Every effort has been made to trace the copyright holders and we apologize in advance for any unintentional omissions. We would be pleased to insert the appropriate acknowledgment in any subsequent edition of this publication.

Endpapers:
Camera Press

Back jacket:
Capital Pictures/ James McCauley

Additional DK photography: Andy Crawford